About the cover - This photo was taken when Rick and I were vacationing on Huron Beach in northern Michigan, June 2014.

A Widow's Words:
Grief, Reflection, Prose, and Poetry
–
The First Year

By Katherine Billings Palmer
TheWritingWidow.com

Copyright © 2019 by Katherine G. Palmer
All rights reserved. This book or any portion thereof may not be reproduced or used in any manner whatsoever without the express written permission of the publisher except for the use of brief quotations in a book review.

Printed in the United States of America

First Printing, 2019

Katherine Billings Palmer
Garden City, MI 48135
katherinep@thewritingwidow.com

www.thewritingwidow.com

To Rick, my love, my life, my soul mate -

Thank you for your never-ending love, compassion, and faith in me...

until I see you again.

- Gerry

ABOUT THE BOOK

How did I end up publishing my most personal thoughts in a book for the world to see? What made me decide to allow total strangers to peek into my heart and glimpse the raw pain and grief that overcame me following my husband's death?

When I began this grief journal, it was out of a survival instinct. I had always attempted to use journaling to sort through my thoughts in an attempt to gain insights into my feelings, to elicit and capture whatever furtive thoughts lurked deep within my mind. For most of my adult life, writing through painful emotional events soothed me. Composing poetry helped me extract and experience all the pain my logical brain kept me from feeling. After my husband's death, writing was all I had.

I met Rick Palmer when I was nearing forty. After a few years of unsuccessful relationships, I was the single mother of one son, and I had given up on ever finding "the one." However, Rick and I knew from the first meeting that it was meant to be, and we enjoyed twenty-one wonderful years together.

Rick was diagnosed with small cell lung cancer in October 2016. By our 20th wedding anniversary the next July, he was in remission, but was suffering from several side effects of the chemo and radiation therapy he had undergone. He died unexpectedly on August 13, 2017, three days after falling and breaking his hip.

Rick and I owned a web design company, and a blog was the natural receptacle for my journal of feelings, thoughts, and memories. It was also the perfect way to honor the man I loved beyond life and a place to dedicate my thoughts, love, poetry, and prose to Rick. However, the blog was private, only shared with my closest friends and family members.

After a few months, I began to share a few of my posts and some of my poetry with other widows in the Hope for Widows Foundation private Facebook group. Group members often responded to my writing by telling me that I put into words what they could not express. Shortly after joining the group, I was honored to be invited to become a guest blogger for the Hope for Widows website. At that point, I made the decision to "go public." I chose a pen name, the Writing Widow, and publicized my website on Facebook, Instagram, and Twitter.

Since opening my blog to others, I have been immensely rewarded with comments and thankyous from many other widows, and those who have lost other loved ones, as well. Several of them suggested publishing my poetry, which I did in, *I Wanted to Grow Old With You: A Widow's First Year of Grief in Poetry*. This book - *A Widow's Words* - is a compilation of my blog posts from the year following Rick's death, including the poetry from my earlier book.

Grief is universal. No two widows grieve in the same way, but, hopefully, my musings will comfort others as they navigate the perilous and emotional journey of widowhood on their own.

Katherine Billings Palmer
TheWritingWidow.com

ACKNOWLEDGMENTS

Following the death of her husband, the widow discovers how truly blessed she is to have friends and loved ones to surround her with love and support. In the week between Rick's death on Sunday, August 13, 2017, and my first entry in this book - August 19th - my niece, Marsha, tended to me as if I was a baby. She cooked for me, cleaned my house, took care of phone calls and arrangements, held me and talked me through what she called "grief contractions," and slept on the couch next to my recliner, where I lay most nights because I was unable to handle sleeping in my empty bed.

In that first week - and month - following Rick's death, while I existed in a fog of grief, my son Brandon took care of the cremation arrangements. Brandon, his wife Lindsey, my stepkids Cindy and George, George's wife Beccy, and Marsha's husband Todd - were all there for me, dropping by, calling, texting, and taking care of memorial arrangements. They surrounded me in a cocoon of love and support, and I couldn't have made it through that awful time without them.

In the year that followed, my friend Walter, whom I have known since I was four years old, let me cry on his shoulder and talk through my grief by cell phone nearly every night. My thanks go out to him, and his husband, Karl, who never complained about my intrusion into their evenings together.

My other oldest pal, Traci, became my weekly dinner companion and another shoulder to cry on. A dear friend I used to work with, Tina, became my "substitute date" for the weekly movie/dinner date nights that I used to share with Rick.

During the twelve months after Rick died, old friends and new sent me cards and Facebook greetings and offerings of support too numerous to list here. My ex-sister in law Linda spent hours beautifying my yard, my nephews and older grandchildren helped with yard work and pool maintenance and moving and lifting things around the house. I lack the amount of space I would need to acknowledge all of those who offered acts of kindness and words of compassion in my first year of widowhood, but I thank them all here for helping me through the worst year of my life.

My friend Jo, whom I've known for nearly forty years, offered to perform the monumental task of editing this book. I know it was a depressing job for her; she, herself, was mourning Rick's loss after years of friendship, and I appreciate the time and effort she put forth to complete the task. Any errors still evident in this book are mine and reflect my own "poetic license."

I am forever indebted for the support and encouragement of these many family members and friends. Thank you all.

And, finally, I need to thank my grief counselor, Vaiva, for her invaluable wisdom and guidance throughout this trying time. She's helped me adapt to widowhood, encouraged me to use my writing to work through my grief, and has worked to help me create a new vision for my future as I continue my life's journey without my husband.

- Katherine

A Widow's Words: Grief, Reflection, Prose, and Poetry - The First Year

Journal Entry From the Night Before You Died	1
Once You Got the Death Sentence	2
Total Eclipse	3
We Did Everything Together	4
Friday, Work at Home Day	6
Pain Menu	8
Evenings Are the Worst	9
Relegated to Photos and Memories	12
Sunday Mourning	13
I knew	14
You're Supposed to Hold Me When I'm Grieving	15
Officially Dead	16
It Isn't Fair	18
Everything Is a Memory	19
Who Am I Mourning For?	22
Life is Easier Now	24
Groundhog Day	25
20 Years	27
Better Off	28
You're Not Coming Back, Are You?	30
I'm Not Normal	31
I Hate Fridays - Post on Hope for Widows Facebook Group	34
I Just Made Eggs for Breakfast	35
Frozen in Time	37
I Just Remembered the Giant TV	38
Horseplay Memories	39
Every Step I Take Forward Is a Step Away From You	40
Wind Phone	41
Living Alone in Our World	44

Our House - the Song	46
Wherever You Will Go	48
My Mother Was Wrong	49
Twelve Weeks	53
Flashbacks	55
Thursday, November 9, 2017	56
Frozen Meat	57
Thoughts This Morning	58
Weeki Wachee	60
I Desperately Want to Turn Back Time	63
Sunday, November 13, 2017	64
The Medical Procedure	66
The Award You Weren't Here For	68
Friday, 11/17/2017	69
Sausage biscuits and bananas...	71
How I Handle Anxiety	71
Taco Bell Hot Sauce	72
Thoughts On My Birthday	73
Three Firsts	75
Home Depot	76
The First Time I Felt Love	79
I Sit Here on a Cold Dark Evening Wondering How I Got Here	81
One More Time	83
I Want to Be Alive Again	85
The Ikea Furniture	87
It's Times Like These	91
Time Hop	95
The Little Losses	96
Sometimes I Wail	97
A Visit From You	102
I Went to Costco Today	103
You Died When I Left the Room	105
Christmas	106

New York Times 2017 "The Lives They Loved"	107
Will You Still Be Here?	109
What If?	111
Picking at the Scab	112
Love Is Not All	117
The New Year	118
In Memoriam	120
I Woke Up Feeling Good Today	122
I Don't Know Where He Is	125
You and I Were a Team	127
If I Don't Grieve You As Hard, Does That Negate Our Love?	130
The Weekend	131
Mask	135
A Special Kind of Lonely	135
Farmington Road	136
The Sadness Is Back	139
Chasing Cars	141
I'm Angry	144
Our Site Gallery	146
The Grief Is Lessening and That Scares Me	149
I Miss My Best Friend	151
Dismembering Your Life	153
Hope	156
Miles - A Poem I Wrote to Rick in May 1996	158
Distance Cannot Stop My Love	159
Our First Date Anniversary	160
I'll Be Seeing You	162
Day Two: Jack in the Box	164
The Dream	168
Distraction	170
August 8th	171
Widow	174
I'm Glad I Made the Trip	177

Who Am I?	179
Trevor Noah on Grief	182
If I Could Have You Back for One Day - A Poem	183
Saturday Afternoons in Bed - A Poem	184
Thirst - A Poem	186
Scraps	188
I Wanted to Grow Old With You - A Poem	190
Time, Grief, and an Apple Watch	191
The Blue Chair: A Widow's Lament	195
The Cure - A Poem	200
The Wind Chimes on the Deck - A Poem	202
It's All Just Attempts at Distraction	204
An Eternity of Sundays Without Him	207
Danger! Grief Triggers Ahead	210
The Tulips in Our Yard - A Poem	213
Vestiges of Your Life - A Poem	216
Sitting Alone at the Coney Island	218
Grief Work: A Job I Didn't Apply For	220
The Legacy of the Do-It-Yourselfer	225
I Want to Keep You Alive	228
Memorial Day Weekend, 2018 - A Poem	230
On Grief and Grandkids	234
A Lifeline of Hope for the Newly Grieving: It Gets Better	239
Alone at the Crossroads	244
See You on the Other Side	247
The Sounds of Silence	250
The Last Spray Bottle	253
The Handprint on the Wall	257
A Year's Worth of Dust and Memories	261
Time on My Hands	266
I Met a Man – A Poem	270
Happy Anniversary to Me	273
In Memoriam: Navigating the Bridge Between "Us" and "Me"	278

It Takes a Village	283
The Dance	288
Garbage Day	292
The Futility of the Physical	298
One Year Without You - A Poem	304
It's Just a Day	308
Happy Birthday to My Love - A Poem	311
Eighty Percent Me	313

Journal Entry From the Night Before You Died

Twenty years. We missed each other for a few, early on, when we lived apart. Why did we waste that time?

I sit here alone in the living room, wishing you were next to me. I dread going to bed, the empty bed.

What a journey we've had. You've taken me to incredible heights and depths. It was a crazy ride. I don't want it to be over yet.

Remission – a beautiful word, yet meaningless? Our new beginning, our bucket list, hasn't happened. Sickness and stupidity – from pneumonitis, to blood clots, to steroid issues, to a broken hip??? Where's the time we are to share and enjoy this respite from cancer?

You are my best friend, so I'm alone. I need you to comfort me at the end of a long day watching you suffer. What a dilemma. Needing you so badly after dealing with your ordeals.

Who will ever hold my hand, stroke me, hear me, the way you do? I need your love and your touch. I need your humor and your intelligence. I need the connection that I've felt for twenty years. I honestly feel like you'd be able to hear me telepathically right now.

Once You Got the Death Sentence

Once you got the death sentence, you said there was nothing we could do about it.

But you didn't die that Christmas, and you didn't die that spring.

And we had time for Christmas with the family.
And spring in Florida.
And – in between hospital visits – we had summer at home.

We had
Time with friends
Time alone
Sunsets and wine and pizza
Sunday mornings in bed
Afternoons in the park
Evenings of hand holding side by side

We had nights of conversation and cuddling.

Once you got the death sentence, we had some extra time. . .

To say goodbye.

August 19, 2017

Total Eclipse

The world talks of the solar eclipse. The day you died, pain eclipsed my world.

August 21, 2017

We Did Everything Together

I sit here mourning your death, and I think, who would understand this pain? We did everything together. Since you retired in 2011, you'd drive me to work in the morning, pick me up and take me to lunch, then pick me up and take me home.

On Fridays, I worked from my home office, and you and I chatted throughout the day.

On weekends, we began every morning with you across from me at a diner table, reading your New York Times, while I sat across from you, doing my crossword, and seeking your knowledge on various arcane or esoteric topics. At the end of the meal, you'd reach across the table and say, "Let the big fella take a look at it." I'd give you the puzzle and jokingly hold back the pen, saying, "You won't be needing this." But you'd take the pen, and you'd fill in some blanks. And I'd scowl, and you'd laugh. Then you'd hand it back and say, "That's why they call me the big fella." And I'd say, "No, it's not." And you'd chuckle.

On Saturday afternoons, we'd do errands, or shop, or look at condos that we'd consider for our future. Or we'd work on our clients' websites – you in your office and me in mine – arguing across the hall about how to proceed on a design, or what the best content writing should be. You'd swear intermittently about some slow-moving software, or some password you forgot, or something that irritated you. And that irritated me. "Just take a break," I'd say. Or "Knock it off; it's not that big a deal. Why do you get so upset?"

And sometimes you'd quit and go into the bedroom to take a nap. And most times I'd join you. And it would evolve into more than a nap. And every time, I appreciated what I had. Time with you. Time to love. Time to talk.

And Sundays were much of the same. Same diner, some errands – or home improvement projects – but we'd always have that afternoon nap. And we'd agree that there was nothing like a Sunday afternoon spent together in bed.

And this last year, after the doctor pronounced the death sentence, I made a point to live every moment. We both knew the end was going to come earlier for you. How long? Every breakfast, I thought, how will I do this without him? Every nap, I thought, hang on tight. Hang on tight. Every errand, I thought, how will I navigate a Saturday alone? Every dinner, I thought, how can I enjoy food that he didn't cook on his precious grill?

My boss let me work from Florida. We had six weeks. We had two long road trips, stopping for Jack in the Box, staying at various motels that you'd rate based on their access to a nice place to sit outside and drink wine. We had day after sunny day, me working in the condo during the day – you'd bring me lunch, or take me to some interesting place you found during your daily travels. We had those nightly Florida sunsets and weekend explorations.

And in those final months, those months I hoped and prayed weren't our final months, as you got weaker and sicker, and you stopped cooking, as you stopped driving, yet seemingly without reason because they said the cancer wasn't back…in those final months, I was able to work from my home office and see you all day, every day. You took lots of naps, but I was here when you awoke. And sometimes, I'd join you on my lunch break, and we'd lay in each other's arms talking. And most days, I'd join you again, the minute I shut down my laptop for the day. You'd say, "Come lay with me." And I would.

You said you didn't really have a bucket list. You didn't want to go back to Europe (although before the death sentence, you said you did). You said you wanted two things: to go on a long road trip and to finish our house and move me into a condo. You wanted to know I was okay after you were gone.

We never got to take that road trip, and you were too sick to work on the house. But that's alright, because I'll never be okay.

We did everything together, and now you're not here. And I grieve, and I wail, and I mourn.

But I try to remind myself that we had years of doing everything together and how very lucky I am that we had that.

August 21, 2017

Friday, Work at Home Day

You're supposed to be in the next room.

It's Friday, work at home day. We're supposed to chatter back and forth all day, you in your office across the hall, me in mine.

But it's silent.

I can't hear your big fingers clacking away at the keyboard – the fastest hunt and peck typing I've ever heard.
I can't hear you groan when your knees creak as you stand, or groan again as you plunk back down into your office chair.
I can't hear you yell, "Kitty, shut up!" as she whines for no reason. Or hear you finally succumb to her plaintive cries and open the back door, only to slam it again with a loud curse (Stupid head!) when she simply stares outside at the yard.

You aren't asking if I want you to make me some breakfast.
You aren't asking, "What's on the agenda for today?"
You aren't there.

You're supposed to be in the next room.

September 1, 2017

Pain Menu

Which memory shall I select? What will bring on the tears?
You at the end? Hooked to monitors, breathing by machine?

You at the beginning? Our first date? Our first kiss?

Or the many options from the 21 years in between?

The memory selection is endless. The choices are triggered with little to no effort.

Choose one, name your poison, pick your pain.

Dancing in the kitchen
Driving in the car
Memorable trips
Weekend excursions

Audio or visual?
Catchphrases and slogans and arguments and endearments
Smiles and scowls and staring into your eyes

Sand and snow
Sun and rain
Us together

"Smell that ocean, honey. Smell that ocean."

Playing Boggle and drinking Peppermint Schnapps

Watching Doc Martin in our ma and pa chairs

Our firsts. Our lasts. Our life. Our love.

September 1, 2017

Evenings Are the Worst

Evenings are the worst.

Coming home from work to an empty house – the new normal.

No plans, no dinner, no evenings on the deck, chatting about our day, drinking wine and eating appies and listening to Five for Fighting Pandora. No watching you prep and grill dinner while I grab a swim. No moving to sit under the gazebo after dinner, the gazebo that you erected on the deck you built, sitting across from you under the blue lights you strung up (because you love blue lights), listening to your ideas and opinions and memories and dreams and plans – and relishing your feedback and comments when I tell you mine.

But then, mornings are the worst.
Waking up alone. No "Gerry, time to get up." No nudge from behind, no

clatter of you wandering around the house, feeding the cat, letting her out, playing at your computer… waking up noises. "Gerry, do you want me to make you breakfast?" Cooking me scrambled eggs. Microwave door slamming as you heat my sausage patty before assembling my to-go breakfast (with cheese sprinkled on top) in a plastic bowl. No more, "C'mon Ger…I'll go warm up the car," and "I've got your computer." And getting into the car with the already-warmed seats and leaning to kiss you good morning.

No, maybe driving is the worst.
One shared car (why would we need two? we did everything together) so you drove me in the mornings, often came back to take me out for lunch, picked me up after my hours were up at the end of the day. Driving everywhere together, to work, to restaurants, to wander around looking at potential condos, through parks, down streets… wandering wandering wandering, which is your favorite thing to do. Me complaining about your attitude behind the wheel (Me – "We're not in a hurry, why do you care how bad the traffic is?" You – "Because it's not right. There are rules."). Me constantly pointing out potential problems to watch for and pissing you off ("I see it, Gerry! I've been driving for years."). You reaching over to try to pinch my inner thigh and me letting out a blood curdling yelp to retaliate. You reaching over to try to grab my nose, but I lick your hand and you pull it back with a disgusted noise. Now I drive alone, no music – can't bear to hear another song that reminds me of you. No silence, can't stand the way I think of you when I see every landmark with a memory behind it. So I listen to the news and miss you next to me every minute of the drive.

Actually, not getting your texts is the worst.
No texts asking, "What time do you want to go to lunch?" No texts asking, "What did you want at Costco?" No texts at 4:30 saying, "I'm here." No texts from outside on the deck to me inside the house. "Are you coming out for a glass of wine?" No texts from the hospital, "I love you, forever." "I miss you." "When are you coming up?"

No, night time is the worst.

No bitching at you when I come to bed and you're wrapped like a burrito in both our blankets. No grabbing my pillow from your arms, where you've cuddled it and made it too warm. ("I want a fresh, cool pillow

– you made it hot!") No hearing you ask, "What time is it?" as I come to bed, or feeling you reach over and with your muscular strong strong arms, simply pull me across the king-sized bed to you. No more of your wonderful, thoughtful, perfect back rubs to help me relax and get to sleep, no more giving you some of the same, and hearing you AAH, and OOH when I hit just the right spot – or YOW when I accidentally touch your sensitive spine. No more touching. No more loving. Night time is the worst.

Saturday afternoons are the worst.
No more, "Let's take a nap," after only lounging around all morning and going to the diner for breakfast. Yup, time for a nap. And if it's a rainy day, you lay on your back and I cuddle on my side, close to you, nestled under your arm, stroking your huge muscled chest. And we talk about plans and life and things we're reading, and our family, and our friends, and our business, and our dreams. And you say, "I love listening to a rainstorm," and "I love listening to the train whistle far away," and "Let's pretend we're sleeping in the back of a pickup truck that we live out of as we wander across the country." Because you were a dreamer. And now you aren't there on Saturday afternoons at all.

Sunday mornings are the worst.
Sleeping in late to find you've been up for hours, but you rejoin me in bed for some cuddle time. You always print my special Sunday NYT puzzle with much bitching about how the printer isn't working right or that the puzzle didn't print large enough. Going to breakfast (again!) at the diner. You read your paper and editorialize on what you've read. You end the breakfast by telling me the Tigers' latest stats – and we both know I don't pay attention, and we both know I'm being facetious when I say, "Oh wow!" and have no clue what the stats mean, and don't care. But you always tell me. And now you don't.

Evenings, and mornings, and driving, and not getting texts, and night-time, and Saturday afternoons, and Sunday mornings are the worst, but, otherwise, I guess I'll be okay without you.

September 2, 2017

Relegated to Photos and Memories

Relegated to photos and memories
You, who were here only weeks ago
No longer tangible, touchable, real

Relegated to pictures and memories
You, who I loved with all my being
No longer here in my bed

Relegated to pictures and memories
Captured digitally and on 4×6 prints
Part of my elusive dreams

September 2, 2017

Sunday Mourning

Tell me again why I should get up today.

To feel more pain?
To feel so lonely it hurts?
To remember again that the person I want to be with more than anyone is gone?

Tell me again that my life should go on.
Tell me he would've wanted it that way.
Tell me again that he's better off, that he would've suffered.

Like I suffer now?

Tell me again that I have things to live for:

a life

a family

grandchildren

a future.

Tell me again because none of that seems to matter when I wake up in my empty bed.

Tell me again that time will heal this awful pain.

Because time is standing still.

September 3, 2017

I Knew

I knew I loved you, but I didn't know how much.
I knew it would hurt when you were gone, but I couldn't imagine this pain.
I knew the house would feel empty, but never thought it would be this quiet.
I knew you were special to me and I was right.

I knew our time was limited, but I didn't know how short.
I knew I would mourn your leaving, but couldn't imagine this level of grief.
I knew enough to cherish each day, but will those memories be enough to last forever?

September 4, 2017

You're Supposed to Hold Me When I'm Grieving

You're supposed to hold me when I'm grieving.

For more than twenty years, your huge warm comforting embrace has been my strength through sadness and despair.

How can I live through losing you?

You were my bulwark.
Your giant strong hands held mine through every loss I suffered, every sadness, every disappointment.

Whose hands will hold mine now?

Your words comforted me through the loss of both my parents, my aunt, our friends, life's lowest points.
Your encouragement kept me strong when I was at my weakest. Your love embraced me through it all.

How can you be gone? Where will I turn now?

You're supposed to hold me when I'm grieving,

But now I'm grieving you.

September 4, 2017

Officially Dead

One by one, form by form, I remove your name from our accounts and you begin to disappear from this world.

No longer joint owner on our bank accounts, credit cards, mortgage, pension.

No longer listed as beneficiary on anything of mine.

Removing your name from each feels like a dagger through my heart.

September 5, 2017

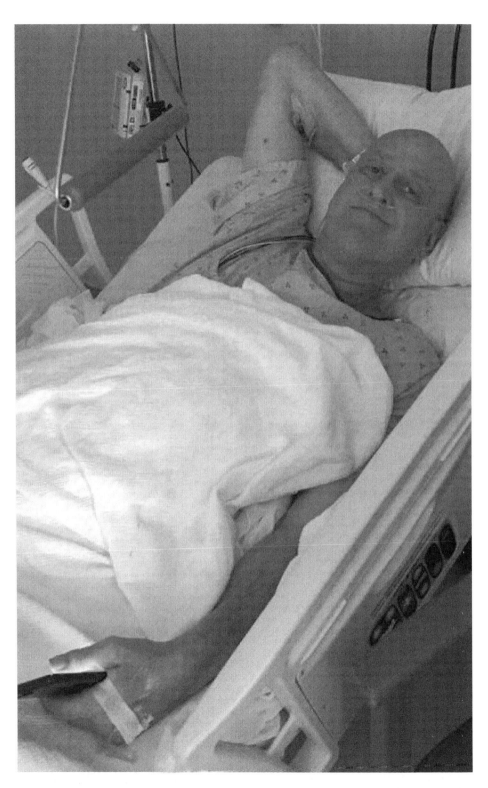

It Isn't Fair

You did everything you were supposed to do.

I asked if you were angry. You said, what can I do? All I can do is what they tell me now.

And you did.

Four rounds of chemo
Pills for nausea
30+ lung radiation treatments
10 brain radiation treatments
Numerous numerous numerous blood tests
3 blood transfusions
Shots for the low white blood count
Steroids for pneumonitis
Shots for blood clots

Jabs and jabs and jabs for more blood tests
Pills for everything in between

You did everything you were supposed to do.
You didn't complain. You didn't cry. You followed every directive, were subjected to CT scans and PET scans and x-rays.
You did everything you were supposed to do and you died anyway.

It's just not fair. You went through too much. You should be here enjoying remission. We should be on our trip across country. You should be by my side.

You did everything you were supposed to do. And you're gone.

September 7, 2017

Everything Is a Memory

It's work at home Friday again. I can imagine you in your office, doing whatever chore is required today to keep the business going. I can hear you asking me, "Is there anything I can do to help?" when I complain that there are too many deadlines and I can't keep up.

I can't go there. I can't start picturing you again, your funny quirky sense of humor, your big, loud, noises as you wander about the house doing mundane things.

Instead, I'll try to stop these thoughts.

I look to my left and notice my copy of Strunk and White's Elements of Style. I remember flying to be with you for a weekend in Minnesota, in the early years, when we had our "telecommuter marriage." I remember telling you I read the entire Strunk and White book on the flight, and when you saw the book you were surprised, because you had pictured an old English classic, like "Humphrey Clinker" and thought I was saying some old geezer's name: Strunken White. And we laughed. And this is just one more stupid memory. One more thing that pops up because I can never ever forget you and all we shared.

Oh look, I can look straight ahead at my "Dead Ophelia" print, hanging on the wall in front of my desk – the one you had framed for me – secretly, as a huge surprise. You chose the perfect wood frame with the perfect mat, with the perfect inset color in the mat. And you gave it to me, and I cried. And you thought I was crying because I didn't like it. And you were chagrined to find out it was because I loved it. Because I knew you loved me. Because you even thought to give me that perfect gift.

So, maybe I can look somewhere else – the lamp that was in your office, but you gave to me because I needed it more? The blue iPad case you bought this spring and that you kept accidentally leaving unzipped so every time you picked it up, the iPad dropped out and you yelled, "FUCK!"?

The little wire bird on my desk with the matching wire candle holder that you bought on one of my birthdays – part of the big bag of goodies that you shopped and shopped for because you loved to give those thoughtful gifts that meant you had been thinking of me everywhere you went shopping that week, searching out each special item. Because you loved me and you constantly showed it.

The hand sanitizer – because your white blood count was low from the chemo, so I populated the house, every flat surface, with a hand sanitizer bottle so you wouldn't get sick and die.

But you died anyway.

There's the shocking pink stapler you bought me in Florida when I was trying to put together paperwork while working at the condo on our first spring trip this year – the one we took after you were pronounced in remission and the final lung radiation was complete, but before the brain radiation started. The pink stapler that I thought. "sheesh, I don't need this big stapler – he always buys too much, too big," but now I love it and it's my special stapler because you bought it for me in Florida on our second from last trip before you died.

Let me not focus on your Palmerworks Design business card – the one where we finally agreed on a logo, because we never agreed on a logo. But then, you always forgot to have them in the car and we always had to give out mine with your number written on it by hand.

God, let my brain stop. Please let these memories take a break, just for a while, just for a half hour. They are incessant. They hurt, yet they feel good, too. Painful pleasure in memories of you.

September 8, 2017

Who Am I Mourning For?

I hear a lawn mower running outside. It's a beautiful (too early) fall day. You would love this. You would love the smell of autumn, and the sounds of the mower outside the window. You would want to take a nap with the window open, curled like a burrito in your old stinky blanket. You would tell me that since you were a child, you enjoyed listening to the sounds outside the window while you slept, including people doing mundane chores, like cutting the lawn.

If it was a weekend, and I was home from work, you would call me to join you in bed. Especially those last few months, when you wanted me to just come to bed with you so often throughout the day. You would call out, "Come lay with me." And sometimes I would. God, I wish I had every time. I would run into that room right now with the slightest invitation, and I would hold you and never let go.

Who am I mourning for? My loss? The absence of you in my life? The part of my life that was wonderful and loving and so much fun. My life with my dreamer of a husband?

Or am I mourning for your losses? For all the days like this that you will never experience again? You loved days like this, and smells like this, and sounds like this. And you should be here. You worked hard for your retirement. You worked hard for a pleasant home. You worked hard on our marriage and our relationship and making a good life together. You worked hard for us to have a future of wandering the country, and the globe. And, in the end, you worked hard to survive, to make it through each day.

And now it's over for you, and it was too short.

And I love you so much. And I want you here so much.

Who am I mourning for? Us.

September 8, 2017

Life is Easier Now

Life is easier now. Since the cancer diagnosis last fall, it's been continuous stress: monitoring, doctor visits, pills, x-rays, tests, scans, chemo, radiation, shots, canes, then walkers. Reading about cancer, and pneumonitis, and blood cells, and medical studies, and alternative treatments. Trying to get you to eat, trying to help you dress and shower, trying to inspire you to get up one more day, trying to make you happy round the clock. Want to go to the park? Need a blanket?

What do you need? How can I help? How can I make you live?

Yes, that's all over. The worries, the constant fear that the next episode will kill you. That you won't make it home from the hospital. That you'll die and leave me.

Yes, that's all over.

Life is easier now, if you don't count the constant pain, the horrible sadness, the emptiness, the loss, the unhappiness, the horrific horrific fear that I will not be able to recover from the pain of living the rest of my life without you.

September 8, 2017

Groundhog Day

My life has become a movie: *Groundhog Day*.

Every morning I wake up and realize you're gone all over again.

I drive in my car on the way home from work, looking forward to seeing you when I get there – oh wait, Rick is dead. I knew, but I forgot.

I walk into my house and suddenly realize the silence. Oh wait, Rick is dead. But I knew that, didn't I?

I'm losing my marbles.

Wait, isn't he in bed waiting for me, as I watch late night TV? Won't I find him there, waiting to pull me into his arms? No, silly, he's dead. He's gone. He's never coming back.

I knew that. Didn't I?

One month, nearly a month you've been gone. And daily, sometimes hourly, I need to remind myself that you aren't coming back. And the pain is unleashed anew – fresh, raw, pain, as fresh as the moment of your death – all over again.

Just like in Groundhog Day, I'm doomed to repeat the reality of your death, the fresh waves of grief.

Look, there's a new sequel to your favorite book series coming out today. Rick will love this, I think. I should call him, I think. But wait, Rick's dead. But I knew that, didn't I?

Over and over and over. I'm reminded that I'll never see you or touch you again. Over and over, I'm hit with a fresh wave of agony, tears and pain. Over and over I see you in my thoughts, I hear you in my dreams, I feel you next to me.

And remember it's not true. You're dead. You're not coming back.

I knew that. Didn't I?

September 12, 2017

20 Years

Two decades in the middle of my life. In time, is that what you'll become? I man I loved for two decades of my life?

Twenty years is so awfully awfully short.
Why does it hurt so much to picture you this way?
To think that some day you'll be a man I once loved?

Will I be an old woman of eighty thinking back to the one special time we shared?
Twenty years, one fourth of my life? Is that all you'll be?

A fading memory?

A special special person I once shared my life and dreams with?

I wanted you forever. I wanted to be old and gray in our matching chairs, watching home shows and Jeopardy until the end.

But no, I'm on my own, and we only had twenty years – two very short decades of love, passionate love, indescribable love.

But only 20 years.

You were a man I once loved.

It hurts to know that's all we'll ever have.

September 20, 2017

Better Off

Jo asked me if I was better off after losing you than I was before we met.

We were talking finances, and the answer is yes.

But how many other ways am I better off today?

You told me so often how intelligent I was, how beautiful, how sexy, how talented. You disparaged others who didn't appreciate me as an employee or coworker or friend.

You gave me confidence in so many ways, over the smallest, oddest things. You considered me a letter writer extraordinaire. You loved my smile. You loved my hair. You encouraged my writing.

When we met, I was a nearly 40-year-old late bloomer, a single mother struggling financially. I was fresh out of the university, only just beginning to earn enough to live on, only recently finding my calling as a writer. I was discovering my independence and beginning to realize my strength – only just finding and becoming myself. Your love, encouragement, and faith in me made me continue to bloom. You made me complete.

Now, here I am, a 60-year-old woman, newly widowed – single again. Financially, yes, I'm better off. Because of how you structured your pensions, I'll have nearly the same income while spending for one, eating for one, living alone. I have choices that I never would have had from living off only my income for the past twenty years. I have income from our business – the business you cultivated and worked so hard to maintain until the month you died.

But I have so so so much more.

I have faith in myself. I believe in myself. I believe I am worthy of the love of a good man. I believe I can write and that I am smart, and that I am special.

I believe all the things you told me about myself.

So, yes, I am better off today financially than the single mother you met more than a decade ago.

But I am also a different person, a better person, a more confident woman. I will forever be the me I have become with your love inside me – a love that is a permanent part of who I am today. I have been forever changed by all you have given me and showed me and by having been loved so very well by you.

September 13, 2017

You're Not Coming Back, Are You?

I think I keep waiting for your return.

Maybe you're at the store. Maybe you even left town for a couple of weeks, as strange as that would be.

Maybe you're off riding your bike…riding, riding…back streets, dirt roads, through the park, enjoying yourself on this beautiful 76° day.

Maybe you're at Costco roaming the aisles, checking out all the prices of the new things you could possibly buy.

Maybe you're not. Maybe you're really not coming back.

Maybe this wounded part of my heart and illogical part of my brain are going to have to grasp the fact that you're not out there somewhere, you never will be coming back.

September 13, 2017

I'm Not Normal

I've never been less normal in my life.

Nothing is appealing – no food, no entertainment, no joy, no hope, nothing. I died when he died.

I try to comfort myself with little "nice" things. I like to sit in my recliner, under his big brown blanket (it's really burgundy; he always called it brown). I like to cuddle up in it, turn on the TV and zone out. Except I don't.

Last night, I watched America's Got Talent. Rick hated AGT and all the other inane shows I enjoyed as brain candy. In one scene, Tyra Banks reached over and ran her hands through Simon Cowell's chest hair. I pictured Rick's thick, sexy gray/white hair peeking out over the V of his shirt. I will never be able to run my fingers through it again. I began to sob.

I want him back. I need him. My heart is broken into tiny bits.

Sunday, I decided he wouldn't want me to be this zombie, this dead woman just existing and performing her duties mindlessly, daily. I decided Rick would want me to eat my low-carb lasagna on the deck in the beautiful summer-like weather. For added enjoyment, I took out a fresh bottle of red wine – from the cases I have left from his memorial "celebration." (Oh, how happy he'd be to see those cases of wine in our basement!)

I cleaned the table on the deck. I took out the food, a crossword, and the wine.

He wasn't there to chat about the day, or make observations about the quality of the wine, or plan what we would do during the week, or just be there, next to me.

I want him back. I can't stand this exile from my soul mate.

September 20, 2017

I Hate Fridays
(A Post to the Hope For Widows Facebook Group)

I hate Fridays! I can't stop sobbing. I want to go out on the deck with my husband and celebrate the end of the work week. We should be enjoying wine and appetizers, then whatever he grilled for our dinner. I want to sit and talk about nothing and everything. Then I want to dance in the kitchen because a song we loved came on the radio. And it's still summer weather here in Michigan and at midnight, I want to skinny dip in our pool.

I can't believe he's gone forever. He died August 13th. This was Rick in April, when our friends let us stay in their Florida condo. They gave us four wonderful weeks of sunsets that I knew we wouldn't see together again next year. He was in remission from small cell lung cancer. He worked so hard – chemo, lung radiation, preventative brain radiation, shots, and transfusions. He was supposed to have at least 9 months until it would surely return with no hope for cure.

We were supposed to have a little more time, but then he got pneumonitis, and then he got blood clots in his lung, and he lost 60 pounds, and he wasn't healing, but he got up every day and tried. He tried so hard to get strong again! And then he fell and broke his femur and it sent fat embolisms to his lung and he died a day later!! The doctors were stunned. I wasn't ready. He can't be gone. I didn't meet him until I was 40 and we had 20 years. It wasn't enough. We were supposed to retire together and travel. My heart physically aches right now. He was my soul mate and my love and I'm trying to fill the hours but I hate Fridays and weekends so much. This site has been my only salvation. Friends and family try to understand but they don't. Thank you for listening and sharing your stories. You have no idea how much you have helped me.

September 22, 2017

I Just Made Eggs for Breakfast

Dear Rick,

I just made eggs for breakfast.

You used to do this for me every day before I left for work. You'd ask, "Do you want breakfast?" and I'd say, "Yes, please." And you'd make three scrambled eggs in a small pan while I showered, and dressed, and ran to catch up because, as usual, I'd overslept.

Meanwhile, you'd already have put a frozen sausage patty in the microwave. When both the sausage and eggs were done cooking, you'd take out a small plastic bowl with a blue lid. You'd layer the sausage on the bottom of the bowl, topped by the egg, topped by some shredded cheddar cheese, then twist the lid onto the bowl and leave it sitting on the island. Then you'd get out a cold Diet Coke and place it next to the breakfast bowl.

When we were leaving for work, you'd say, "I'm going out to start the car.
I've got your laptop. Don't forget your breakfast."

It's the memories of those mundane things in life that are the killers. The memories that make me want to drop to my knees in grief. The small kindnesses you performed for me all day, every day, every week, every month, for 21 years.

The simplicity of what you did in that five minutes as you prepared my breakfast and left the house speaks volumes. You loved me. You cared. You'd do the smallest loving acts of kindness, just to make my mornings easier. Just because you were you.

(And you knew just how much I hated mornings. You knew because you were my human alarm clock, my human snooze button, reminding me every ten minutes, "Gerry, get up." "Gerry, it's getting late.")

I got up on my own this morning. I made my own breakfast. I didn't want to eat, but hunger finally overtook the lethargy. I don't ever want to eat again, to be honest. I don't want to get out of bed in the morning, shower, dress. I just want to disappear. I want to reappear wherever you are, and just be with you forever.

But I made a sausage and egg breakfast because I knew you'd want me to. I will live because I know you want me to. I will go on, but I will never forget the warmth of your love. I will go on, but I will never stop loving you.

October 6, 2017

Frozen in Time

Dear Rick,

Since you died, I've been amassing photos, videos, and even one voice recording I found. I've found things you've written – in longhand – and in Google Docs or Word.

I've gathered anything and everything that can keep your memory fresh.

Right now, I'm doing an Amazon Prime photo backup and seeing pictures I haven't seen in a few years, or never noticed before because finding every possible scrap of you and our life together wasn't as imminently important to me before.

I've gotten the old video cassettes out. They're sitting with my video camera by the iMac, awaiting the time I'll get to them to digitize and store them in the cloud so I'll never lose them.

I'm scouring the house for every tiny insignificant scrap of you that I can keep forever in memory.

And just now, it hit me, once again, that there will never be a new photo, video, handwritten note, audio recording. You've been frozen in time. All I have now is all I'll ever have of you. And, once again, I am incredibly sad that we will never make a new memory, never create a new photo, never speak or see each other again.

Is it me or you who is frozen in time?

October 7, 2017

I Just Remembered the Giant TV

Dear Rick,

I just remembered the giant TV. We bought it at Best Buy after my parents said we could borrow their empty Discover card. You were flabbergasted that they would come down and offer it to us. They lived in the apartment a few doors down and they came to visit just to offer the card. They knew we wanted a TV (well, you and Brandon did).

We drove to Best Buy in the Tracker. You never considered having things delivered because 1. We were always broke and 2. You were strong and did it all yourself.

We had to remove the box to fit it in the Tracker. We even had to remove the vinyl top to even be able to fit the TV. We had to lower in through the bars down into the back seat.

IT WAS HEAVY.

Then we had to get it back out of the car at the apartment and get it into the living room. That TV was moved from Best Buy to the apartment, from the apartment to your friend Lester's, when we decided to buy his house, from Lester's to your mom's for storage, when we decided not to buy the house and Brandon and I stayed with my dad in his apartment. I think we left it at your mom's until we were ready for it in Maryland, then moved it there. Six years later, we moved it back to our new home in Garden City.

IT WAS HEAVY AS HELL.

Eventually, we took it to my dad's apartment in Westland for him to use, since he only had smaller TVs and they were up north.

My dad died and we sold it (for very cheap – we wanted it gone!). You were so excited when the three men came for it were thrilled to death to get this giant TV. You always like it when we had a happy buyer for our stuff. You loved the idea of being generous and making someone happy.

October 17, 2017

Horseplay Memories

Getting on the elevator at the medical center,
you turn to me and jab at my stomach

and I warn you that there are cameras watching your abuse.

Then we continue with the horseplay -

I swat at you
Or I throw my arms around you
And kiss you

Just to give "them" a good show

It became our usual routine alone on that elevator...
daily...
weekly...
more treatments,
more radiation,
more blood draws,
more crap that you endured.

We endured.

How can that most horrible year be something I miss now?

Because I'd take anything, endure it all again,

just to be with you.

October 19, 2017

Every Step I Take Forward Is a Step Away From You

Every step I take forward is a step away from you.

But is it?

It's a step away from what we shared.
It's a step away from my time with you.

But is it also a step toward the future - the afterlife - I will share with you?

Are you sitting on the beach waiting for me, an empty chair, an empty glass on the table next to you?
Are you waiting to sit together and talk over our memories and the time we had together?
Are you waiting, as you so often did out under the gazebo?
Are you waiting for me to join you for eternity?

Then every step I take is a step towards that time we will share forever.

I can't wait to see you again, to touch you again.

In the meantime...
I will miss you and love you and talk to you.
I will create more stories to share with you

When I see you again.

October 22, 2017

Wind Phone

I haven't written to you in a while. I've been talking to you all the time, though. We sit here chatting every evening, don't we? You typically have nothing to say, but we both know I did most of the talking anyway.

I miss you.

Those words sure don't convey the pain of it.

I had a little meltdown this morning. I had one yesterday morning, too. And last night. It seems to be getting worse, not better.

I tried to stop taking the Xanax yesterday. Maybe that caused Meltdown 1. Who knows? I woke up at 7ish and lay in bed thinking about you and crying. Then I read some posts in the widows' groups on Facebook. Somewhere, one of the things I read mentioned a This American Life podcast about a wind phone. Did you listen to that? I wish I would have listened to more of these podcasts when you were alive and listening to them, too. We could have shared more conversation about the responses they all invoke.

This one was about a man whose uncle died in the tsunami in Japan in 2011. In his grief, he bought a telephone booth and put it out in his yard, overlooking cliffs. He sat in it and called his dead relative and talked

to him. Soon, people from all over would come and talk to their loved ones. You probably listened to it.
One in particular really hit me...

The father
One call I watched was from a young father with rectangle glasses and a long black jacket.
He lost his family; both parents, a wife named Mine and a one year-old son named Ise.
"Dad? Mom? Mine? Ise? It has already been 5 years since the disaster.
If this voice reaches you, please listen.
Sometimes I don't know what I am living for.
Ise, please let me hear you call me 'papa.'
Even though I built a new house…
Dad, mom, Mine and Ise without all of you it is meaningless. I want to hear your reply but I can't hear anything."
He takes off his glasses and covers his eyes with his hands.
"I'm sorry. I'm so sorry I couldn't save you."

Oh God, those words.

I'm so so so sorry. I'm so so so sorry I couldn't save you, Rick.

I tried so hard. Every day for months. I tried to help you mentally, tried to help you physically. Tried to save you.

And I failed.

I know it's illogical. I know I'm not God. But, I tried everything I could think of and failed.

In the last few months, you asked me to come lay with you often throughout the day – on my lunch hour, when I finished work at 4, and in the evening, when you went to bed at 9 or 10 p.m.. You wanted to lie next to me and talk, and touch, and just be together. I'm so sorry for every time I didn't.

Sometimes I'd need to finish something, or sometimes I'd be exhausted from caring for you and I'd say I need some alone time – I'll come to bed soon.

I hate myself for that – for not seeing that there wouldn't be much more time, for not recognizing how very sick you were.

I've got plenty of alone time now.

I know I'm human. I try to forgive myself for things that I did because I was tired, scared, and so very sad watching you die.

I know you forgive me. I need to forgive myself.

I love you and always will. That bullshit phrase from the movie, Jerry McGuire isn't bullshit. You complete me. Or you did.

And now I am no longer whole. I am shattered in pieces. I have no choice other than to call up every memory of you and try to savor it forever.

Where are you? If I built a wind phone, could I talk to you?

October 29, 2017

Quote from *This American Life*, Transcript 597: One Last Thing Before I Go
https://www.thisamericanlife.org/597/transcript

Living Alone in Our World

Dear Rick,

We were in a world of our own, a perfect world we created together.

Perfect.

We jealously guarded the world, only letting in close family members. Only going to a few social events if they really struck our fancy. Otherwise, our home, our car, our forays to diners and restaurants were solo. They were us.

We refined our world, we decorated the home, we filled it with the electronics we needed for our web design, our hobbies.

We filled our world with our own books, music, and even TV shows. All the entertainment was culled from things we enjoy together.

And those things that we didn't both enjoy, we enjoyed side-by-side. You reading your iPad, me doing genealogy on my MacBook. We even played Scrabble on our electronic devices, both of us nudging each other ever so often – electronically and verbally. C'mon, are you ever going to make a word?

We enjoyed breakfast at diners, yet rarely communicated. You read your New York Times. I did the puzzle you had printed for me before we left home. I'm sure waitresses thought we one of those married couples who barely spoke. But we didn't need to speak, not at breakfast when we didn't want to. We had refined the communication. We needed few words to communicate to each other.

You drove me to work, you picked me up, and took me to lunch, you drove me home. In our world. Our very special world together.

Oh, every once in awhile I did my thing. I went and played cards, and Friday nights sometimes you went to visit your friends. Once you even went to Arizona for a weekend without me. But even then our world didn't disconnect. Even then we texted and talked and FaceTimed while we were apart.

I went to work at my own job and you stayed home to do websites. During the day, you did your wandering. You loved your wandering time – for those few hours before and after lunch anyway. You liked to eat McDonald's breakfast with a donut at the end. I hated that you did that, Mr. Type 2 Diabetic.

Yes, we did socialize, usually family events, every once in awhile with friends, but usually it was just us. Usually it was just us, and now it's just me. How will I overcome this loneliness? How will I live in our world without you? How?

October 29, 2017

Our House – The Song

Our House
Crosby, Stills & Nash, 1970

Dear, Rick,

I heard "Our House" on the radio yesterday. Of course, I cried. I remember dancing with you in the kitchen when the song came on. I was so happy that we had our perfect life in our perfect house.

But then I remembered earlier, before we met. I remember in the 70s and 80s hearing this song and having such a longing for the picturesque and romantic life described by the lyrics. I wanted this so badly – to be loved by a man and to live happily with that man who loved me.

And it happened. I found this bliss I sought for so many years.

Yes, it's over. But I HAD it. How many people never did? How easily it could have passed me by. Instead of being a widow mourning her loss, I could be a still single "old maid," who'd never enjoyed those fantastic, beautiful, wonderful years with you.

Our time in Maryland seems like a dream now. The house, the toiling, the beauty that resulted from our very, very hard work. I remember sitting in the family room, by the fireplace we built – we didn't have long. Not long after the work was done, we sold the house and moved on. But we enjoyed the kitchen and the family room for more than a year.

And the yard, the beautifully landscaped yard. You built the decks, assembled the fountain, planted the flowers that bloomed all around us as we sat under the gazebo strung with tiny lights, or sat by the fire in the outdoor fireplace – I had all that, and 10 more years of the same when you replicated our garden paradise here in our Michigan home.

I had our house (our very very very fine house) times two.

I had a man who loved me above all else, who lived to make me happy.

I had a man who danced with me to this song – and so many others – in our kitchen.

October 31, 2017

Wherever You Will Go

There are songs I've always liked that take on a whole new meaning now that Rick is gone. It may be wishful thinking, but I feel like he's still near me, loving me, and I try to do what I think he'd want me to. The song "Wherever You Will Go," by the Calling, was mentioned on one of the Facebook widows' groups, and I gave it a new listen. I find it comforting.

Rick was a strong man and he loved me. I want to believe his love is strong enough for this…

…Maybe, I'll find out a way to make it back someday
To watch you, to guide you through the darkest of your days

Rick, are you watching me? Are you guiding me?

November 4, 2017

Songwriters: Aaron Kamin / Alex Band
Wherever You Will Go lyrics © BMG Rights Management US, LLC

My Mother Was Wrong

"A man will never love a woman as much as a woman loves a man." – A quote from my mother after one of my boyfriends left me when I was in my early twenties.

If my mom were here now, I'd tell her how wrong she was.

Richard Kevin Palmer loved me as much as I loved him. He proved that love to me daily. He expressed his love for me better and more vocally than I did in return.

Rick showed me his love with his words. Rick spoke to me of his love often. He could humble me with a few well-chosen words, words of love and adoration.

He told me I was beautiful thousands of times in our 21 years together. He told me how smart I was, and how talented. He boasted about me to his friends – about how I handled the technology in the business, about how well I could write. He expressed his love so often, that I was often speechless in return.

Rick showed me his love with his gifts. He constantly bought me little gifts, trinkets, and surprises – sometimes the dumbest things – and those were the ones I loved the best. The blue china cow from the Mall of America – with white clouds instead of spots? What did that even mean?

Sometimes the gifts did have meaning, elicited memories. The Route 66 tote bag – because we had driven Route 66 together on one of our trips.

He brought me barbecue sandwiches from Memphis wrapped in paper and stuffed in his blazer pocket. He brought me Jack in the Box tacos from California that he'd picked up on his way to the airport where he caught the red eye to Detroit.

Rick showed me his love through his actions. We had known each other only a few months when we went to a barbecue. He brought me a plate of food, and I was amazed to see he knew exactly what I liked. No one had ever done that for me before, but he had watched me on other occasions and knew in our short time together that I liked only mustard on my hot dogs and knew that I didn't like pepper.

Rick did all the grocery shopping. He knew I hated it. He asked me each day what I wanted for dinner, then bought any necessary groceries, prepared the food, and cooked it when we got home – after he had picked me up from work.

We were together as often as possible. He drove me to work in the morning, often picked me up and took me to lunch, then came back to drive me home. We texted throughout the day. We spent our weekends doing everything together.

My first indication of the kind of man Rick was occurred when we were first dating. We were visiting his mother one evening. She was complaining…and complaining….and complaining about something. I can't recall what had upset her. Rick and I were sitting together on the couch, and – after a few minutes of her whining – he reached over and started rubbing the back of my neck. He had the largest hands I've ever seen. Seriously, powerful huge hands that complemented his size 14 feet. He was strong, insanely strong, and he was gently kneading my neck, upper back, and shoulders with those powerful hands. I thought I'd died and gone to heaven.

Later, when we were in the car, I thanked him for the back rub. He told me he felt so bad that I had to listen to his mother's unpleasantness that he was trying to make it up to me.

I received many many more of those back rubs throughout the years. I'd come to bed late, and he'd awaken and reach over to stroke my back. He'd know when I was stressed because of work deadlines or life events and give me a thorough massage without prompting. He'd stroke my head when we lay in bed together on weekend afternoons, just talking and whiling away the hours.

Rick continued to show me love, tenderness, and kindnesses throughout our twenty year marriage. Over the next twenty years without him, I will do my best to remember every single act of endearment and write it down, so I will never forget him or his legacy of love.

Rick was known throughout his life as the Gentle Giant. He loved me with a gentleness and treated me with such kindness, that I know without a doubt he loved me as much as I loved him.

Sorry, mom, but you were very wrong.

November 4, 2017

Twelve Weeks

Dear Rick,

Twelve weeks.

This is the longest we've been apart since the night we met. How can I go on without you?

I thought the pain might be getting better...that the hole in my heart would start to heal. Scar over.

It's not happening. It's getting worse.

Another Sunday morning without you – what do I do? Where do I go? Do I eat my solitary breakfast here at home? Make some eggs and bacon, set up the little table in front of my "cocooning chair" and do my puzzle?

I haven't been out of the house since Thursday night. I'm not sure which is worse. Going out without you or sitting in this tomb of my own making.

It's comfortable, yet painful. I go through pictures and videos and files that are evidence of things we shared – trips and home improvements and all the various business we took care of together. I work to clean out the folders and files and get everything sorted out in case I decide to move, or I happen to die, too.

It needs to be done, this cleansing process. You wanted to help me "get the house cleaned out" and move to a smaller place – a condo – so you would know I'd be okay if – or when (but we didn't say that) you died.

We made this plan before the medical problems started up. We made the plan when we thought we had more time. I remember saying that it wouldn't be fair to you to spend time cleaning out a garage if you didn't have much time. I remember getting up on Saturday and Sunday mornings and saying let's do whatever you want to do today, and we wandered around town, eating breakfast and lunch in restaurants, shopping for nothing we needed, looking at condos, going to parks. Or we hung out around the house, reading, working on websites, napping. So it didn't get done.

And now that you aren't here, I'm glad it didn't get done. I'm glad that we didn't spend that precious, short, short, time cleaning out the crap. I have nothing but time now, honey, time I need to fill with something.

And I'm not sure I even want to leave this place that we shared and move farther away from your memory.

But every shred of paperwork in these filing cabinets reminds me of something we shared and that you're gone forever. Every bin I open has some remnant of you that seems unbearable to part with.

So I entomb myself and clean and sort and cry and remember and cry some more.

It's Sunday morning and I need to decide again. Stay in and work and cry? Or go out to our favorite diner and eat alone and cry when I get back to the car?

Whatever I do, I'm reminded that it will never be the same. I need to go on. You aren't coming back. And the more time passes, the farther away you go, frozen in time. And the more it hurts.

It's not healing. The wound is still gaping open and my life's blood continues to pour.

Twelve weeks is not enough to heal the hole in my heart.

I love you and miss you, Rick Palmer. My soul hurts.

Your wife (and I always will be),
Gerry

Sunday, November 5, 2017

Flashbacks

Dear Rick,

I was taking a quick break to read emails between projects at work. One email was about SAE logo merchandise for sale.

I was browsing through the shirts and suddenly flashed back to Florida – you and I in a Walmart. You were buying two or three of those silky zip-up shirts that you liked so much. You always wore them when riding your bicycle. You convinced me to buy some in my size. (In fact, when we were back in Michigan, after no success finding more at the local Walmart, I ordered more for you online, because you liked them so much and wore them daily.)

The flashback was really of no big memorable activity, just a very small reminder of a typical activity on a Saturday in Florida – our very favorite place to be.

The times we had in Florida were heaven sent. We were so happy there. I am so thankful that we had many weeks before it all went downhill – before the pneumonitis set in, before you lost weight, lost energy, slept more, couldn't walk, got sicker.

Picturing that one Walmart scene brought back Florida in an instant. It brought you back to life. It hurt.

I went to the company's nursing room because the pain was so vivid, I thought I would sob out loud in my cubicle.

The flashbacks are getting stronger and coming on more suddenly now. Or is it that the fog of constant pain has lifted, so when it returns so suddenly, I'm not ready, and it's like a punch to the gut?

I miss you, I miss you so much. I want you back.

November 7, 2017

Thursday, November 9, 2017

Dear Rick,

There are so many things that I wish you were here for. I think you would have been pleased to see me out with your daughter Cindy and our grandkids the other night. I think you would be happy that we are doing Thanksgiving together this year, even though you are gone. They are and will be my family forever. I feel a connection to you through them, and that will hopefully never change.

I wish you could see the fall colors and enjoy this autumn – as you did, while I hated it! Winter is coming. BAH.

I still love you with all my heart.

Gerry
XXOO

Frozen Meat

It's noon and I'm hungry so I went to find food. I thought I'd take out some frozen chicken and maybe make a stir-fry for dinner.

I found 2 frozen chicken breasts and what looks like frozen steaks. Then I found 2 larger bags, with big cuts of some kind of meat.

I thought, this is ridiculous. It looks dry/frosty, and I don't even know what it is or what he was going to cook with it.

Maybe it's for pot roast? Or that thing he made me in the crock pot? What was that? The roast with the garlic slits, and some carrots, onions, and celery? Used to be little potatoes, but we switched to radishes to be keto.

Anyway, I decided the meat is probably pretty old and dried out and I'll just toss it. I said, a quiet, Sorry, honey. Sorry I'm wasting food you bought. Rick hated wasting food, and so do I.

And then, quite suddenly, I couldn't do it. I started to sob. I love him. He's gone. He's never going to cook dinner again. He's never going to shop for some meat, the type he bought, the way he used to price things at different stores. He's not coming back.

I can't do it. I can't throw away this meat he bought, he touched, he planned to use – and use in a dish that he knew I'd especially love. Because that's how he was, so kind to me, always trying to make me happy.

I put it back. I can't throw it out. I'll use it, find a way to figure out what it is and find the recipe he would have cooked and use it.

But it's not going in the garbage today.

November 10, 2017

Thoughts This Morning

Dear Rick,

I watched Danielle this morning – your job. I got up at 6:30am and, while she watched TV, I went into your office and uploaded the Michigan From the Heart website photos – your job.

I drove Danielle to school – your job.

As I was driving down Harrison, I thought how odd it was, this strange loop of life. I used to work at her elementary school. I was a single mother, dreaming and longing for that perfect man to come along, so I could have someone who loved me, who I loved in return.

And now, that love has come and gone, and I was driving our granddaughter – the child of his son – to that same school.

I had that dream so long ago, while working at that very school, and now you're gone. But I had it. I lived the dream. I had those 21 years with you.

It's just so odd, to be driving your child's child to that very school. To now have your family as mine, so many years later. And to have you no longer be with me to share my life.

I can't even really explain the meta thoughts.

Then I drove back to our home, without you in it, and made my breakfast – your job.

Before work, I posted a blog about the Garden City Business Alliance Trunk or Treat – I copied the blog you wrote in 2015 and changed it a bit. But they were your words, and I loved them. And once again, I was doing your job.

And now I sit here alone, without you across the hall.

There's a GCBA meeting today. You aren't here to go to it and come back to tell me all that's going on. The last one you attended, you came back and said one of the members had offered to drive you, because you looked so bad.

The printer just did that warm up sound again - the thing that happens once in a while that I'm convinced is a sign from you.

Are you here? Or am I just a nut widow?

November 10, 2017

Weeki Wachee

I was looking for a picture of Rick cooking to go with a blog post. I came across several pictures from Weeki Wachee. We stayed at a motel, loved it, and Rick went to the park to cook food while I worked during the day.

I knew we had some shots of us at the park. We were alone there, and had completely taken over many of the tables under a gazebo. We each had our own "work" table – me to work on the day job, him to work on websites, plus he had a "food prep" table, and then we had the table where we actually ate the dinner. It was humorous and just the kind of fun we always had together.

I didn't find those pictures, at first. Instead, I found some photos of us outside the hotel room, eating at our little portable work tables. Rick had bought them for us so we could always work on the road.

I had completely forgotten that Rick had made us steaks and portobello mushrooms – at a motel! He was the consummate "work-around" kind of guy – and he did love his food! I had bought him a portable grill that supposedly didn't get too hot and could be used anywhere – and he loved to use it on our trips.

Of course, I felt that bittersweet emotion – joy at the time we shared, devastation that he is gone. Our time is over. He will never go to Florida with me again. He will never make a steak dinner. I don't know if I will ever stop crying.

November 11, 2017

I Desperately Want to Turn Back Time

I desperately want to turn back time.

I want to relive every moment, good and bad.
I want you here.
I want more time.

I want normal and nothing has been normal since you died.

When you were diagnosed, we knew there was no forever,
but I never really pictured it. It was a vague shadowy future that I dreaded but wouldn't allow myself to truly envision.

I couldn't have if I tried.

I never could have imagined a pain this raw.

November 13, 2017

Sunday, November 13, 2017

I had another slight meltdown today after Lynn left. I didn't feel like doing anything except sitting in my Rick blanket cocoon. I guess it was because I spent the entire day until 1:30am with others and didn't have any time to cry.

I thought of Rick several times yesterday. In the movies, he was always next to me. We held hands, shared popcorn and gave each other looks of approval or dismissal after every preview. And this is only the second time I've gone without him after several years of weekly movie dates. It just felt wrong.

Then Jim and Karl joined Wally, Traci, Lynn and me for dinner. Rick should have been there.

Lynn and I had long discussions both last night and this morning. Widowhood, dating, going on alone, hanging onto sentimental things. I think I just was overloaded with emotional thoughts by the time she left.

I sat in my chair and looked over at the couch, just longing to see Rick lying there as he did sometimes, especially in the last months of his life. I passed football games while channel surfing and wished he were here on the rare Sunday afternoon he watched a football game – the special ones, at least.

My life is so empty now. The house is so empty. God, it's awful. I just kept thinking that I can't do this, but I have no option BUT to do it.

Tonight, I watched Curb Your Enthusiasm without him. He would have loved some of these jokes. Larry was dating a woman with a son, and for the first time, it hit me that Rick made the decision to date a woman with a 14-year-old son! I had never looked at that with that perspective before. That's a huge decision. He married me and became a stepfather to a potentially live-in child, even though we never did live together "too much" with him here because of our weird commuter marriage.

It's just odd that I never thought of this with this perspective and from the point of view he may have had. I don't think I would want to date a man who had minor children right now. He made the choice to love me despite the fact that he didn't want to father more children.

So, I had a sort of "emotional "flu" day. I didn't do any of the chores I need to, didn't work on the website updates I need to, nothing. Just sat and cried and watched a movie and ate sandwiches. Then napped a bit. I felt incapable of doing anything else. I'm still devastated by my loss. I love and miss him madly.

I did look at some future travel ideas with the Road Scholars: genealogy and writing trips to Indiana and Wisconsin. I felt some interest, some hope that I could do a couple of these week-long trips. After that was when I lost it again emotionally and started sobbing. Two steps forward, one step back? I picture a future without him, enjoying myself by myself, then feel like I've pushed too far, have left him and our love behind. I don't want to leave him. I can't betray him by having a life without him. That's stupid and I know he wouldn't want that. I can't help how I feel.

My grief counselor said to picture our life together using a metaphor of a beautiful vase we both loved and bought and admired, but that had now fallen and smashed to pieces. I should select some of the beautiful shards and use them to create a lovely mosaic. One of the pieces of the metaphorical vase that I would put in my mosaic is the ability to have the independence to travel, the wanderlust he inspired in me, and the confidence that I could do that by myself. I was becoming more confident before I met him, just by what I accomplished at U of M, but traveling the US, Canada, and Europe with him, gave me even more confidence and the open-mindedness that I could do it alone. Our travels and love of travel will go into the mosaic, and I'll think of him as I wander anywhere in the future.

On the practical side, he taught me how to navigate flying standby as a nonrevenue flyer, get a rental car, and mundane things that are normal for many adults, but that I had never done. I'd driven places with Brandon and gotten hotel rooms, but only a few times. After 21 years of travel, I'm so much more adept and open to going places that I will take that as one of the beautiful pieces of life he gave me.

Oh God, Rick, you were so good to me. I love you so much.

The Medical Procedure

I went for minor surgery without Rick yesterday. He was always by my side, even in the doctor's office when discussing the procedures or issues. He drove me, sat with me, took me for lunch somewhere to celebrate the fact that I had done whatever was required despite my negative feelings about anything to do with doctoring or medicine. I've always been medical-phobic, ever since being raised by a hypochondriac mother. I've gone more than 10 years at a time without tests or doctor visits… until age started affecting my organs and maturity dictated that I need to get the usual checkups and tests.

He was there every step of the way, holding my hand.

Yesterday, he wasn't.

Once, during the summer, near the end of his life, I had to go for a procedure without him. He was having some type of mental issues. He was in the hospital, getting weaker every day, barely able to walk, and quite suddenly, he began to become very dependent and clingy. He was no longer Rick. I'm not sure it was the effects of the brain radiation or just that in-hospital mental confusion that sometimes affected many of my other "older" relatives, but he was not the Rick I knew and loved.

I received strange texts from him, barely legible pleas for me to come be with him. I reminded him that I was at the doctor's office, but that I'd get there as soon as I could. When I arrived at the hospital, our daughter-in-law Beccy was there talking to him. He looked up at me from his bed, saw me in the doorway, and started to sob. I ran to him and hugged him and he grabbed on and wouldn't let go. He was like a child, and my heart hurt to think of him like that. My big strong husband was like a baby in my arms.

He eventually returned to himself, once we got him home, but he still had episodes where he was confused, disoriented, talking jibberish. It reminded me of my dad in the later stages of Alzheimer's and it only added to the sadness and confusion that I felt watching him decline – first physically and now mentally. My Rick was slowly fading away.

And now he's gone. And I'm alone. And I had my first minor surgery without him at my side. Brandon took me, and that also caused some mental adjusting on my part. I'm too young for my children to start taking care of me. All this "new normal" stuff is tough on the brain.

November 15, 2017

The Award You Weren't Here For

I won an award at work today and you weren't here to share the joy with me. You were here when I found out I was being nominated. I just assumed you'd be here to find out if I won.

I'll use the money toward the MacBook you insisted I need. You were planning to buy it for our anniversary in July, but you were too weak to walk into the Apple Store to help me try them out. We went to Best Buy once and you barely made it to the computer section with your walker, stopping to sit in the collapsible seat along the way. A store employee saw how bad you looked and brought you a cup of water. That was nice, heartwarming, but so so awfully sad – watching you sit sipping on a cup of water, looking 80 years old.

I think that was about a week before you died. I remember we went to that new restaurant that serves brunch. In fact, I think that was right after you had your old-fashioned shave at the barber.

Yes, a shave, an abbreviated trip to Best Buy to look at MacBooks, then brunch at the new diner. I have pictures on my iPhone from that day – Saturday, August 5th. You died eight days later.

I'm going to use the award money for the MacBook you tried to buy me for our 20th anniversary. I'm probably going to cry when I buy it, then cry every time I use it – at least for awhile.

Oh God, how I miss you. I love you. I always will. I wish you were here with me to share in this tiny bit of happiness. I wish this tiny bit of happiness actually made me feel happy, but nothing really does anymore. My happiness died with you.

Love,
Gerry

November 15, 2017

Friday, 11/17/2017

Dear Rick,

I think of that broken vase analogy often now. Which beautiful pieces should I pick out to use in a mosaic? What to take from our marriage on my new solo journey – my very painful foray into the future without you?

It's work-at-home Friday. I toiled all morning on a project and finally finished at 2 p.m.. I decided to go to lunch, just get out of the house. What would Rick do? He'd say, "c'mon, let's go to lunch."

You couldn't be contained in a house for long. You used to laugh at me when I said a perfect weekend was not having to go out for anything, no groceries, no reason to leave the house. The thought of going out to run an errand was no thrill to me. But to you, you loved it. You enjoyed wandering and shopping and just getting out.

I will never enjoy errands like you did, but I can at least attempt to enjoy something, anything, again. Since you died, nothing at all is enjoyable. Oh, sure, I went to a movie last night, and it was nice, but there's this overlay of sadness that I can't shake. I can't FEEL. I can't rise above this. You are gone, forever. I will never be the same.

The past couple of days, I didn't think of you constantly. At first, I thought, oh, it's getting better. But I'm not that foolish anymore. This has happened before, this small respite from the pain, and then suddenly WHAM! It'll hit worse than ever.

So, I dressed, left the house, and decided to go to Olga's. You never liked Olga's and we only went there that one time last year. It was safe! No memories of you sitting across from me.

I did a crossword, ate my snackers, and then noticed the music – nothing terrible, no great reminders of you like Paul Simon, or songs about being in love, but they were songs that were popular over the summer, our last summer. They had no more meaning than that. We drove places and those songs came on the radio, and it was all I could do not to break down sobbing in Olga's.

I handled it. I finished lunch and left the restaurant. I was on empty, so I went to the Kroger gas station next door, one you've gone to many times. And I pumped my own gas. You always pumped the gas, Mr. Gallant Husband. And I didn't cry. But I wanted to.

And I got back in the car and sobbed all the way home.

Because you are gone, and I know it, and I can't stand it.

So, I'll continue to try to pull out the pretty, shiny pieces from the shattered vase of our marriage. I'll get out of the house and run errands and try to find the joy you used to have in those small actions.

I'll try to take life easier – try not to fret about everything like I always have, while you tried to make life more enjoyable for both of us, always, with little trinkets, lunches, road trips, just being and doing and not always accomplishing what's supposed to be done.

I love you, honey. I love how enjoyable you made our lives – my life – in all those thoughtful ways.

I'm going to go on without you, but I don't know how yet.

November 17, 2017

Sausage Biscuits and Bananas…

Sausage biscuits and bananas…

The Alexa shopping list still has items I was going to buy for Rick.

It's been fourteen weeks since he died.

November 19, 2017

How I Handle Anxiety

Rick's death changed everything. Okay, so I can be extreme…

Now if I get some weird bill in the mail or some stressful thing happens, I ask myself, what's the worst that could happen?

The man I love more than anything in the world will die and I will miss him constantly? Oh yeah, that already happened, so what could possibly be worse about a stupid fucking bill?

There, how's that for a glass half full?

November 19, 2017

Taco Bell Hot Sauce

Dear Rick,

My coworker Matthew stopped by my desk to discuss hot sauce. He mentioned remembering that Brandon had been saving Taco Bell taco sauce packets at one time.

Wow….remember when Brandon saved hot sauce packets and put them in a giant box and wrapped and gave it to you for Christmas? God, that was funny. You were genuinely thrilled to receive a giant box of Taco Bell hot sauce, that's how much you loved it.

No matter what you were eating, you'd pull out a couple of packets and liberally drench the food – hamburgers, chicken, whatever…you'd add that hot sauce. And it couldn't be "mild" or "fire." It had to be good old "hot" Taco Bell taco sauce.

There were always packets in the car glove compartment, next to your keyboard on your desk, in your backpack, and sometimes in your computer case.

I miss you and your damn quirky ways, you and your hot sauce packets.

November 21, 2017

> As the sun slips below the horizon, drawing the covers over another day, I remind myself that you, like the sun, are still out there... just out of sight. And maybe this night, I'll see you again in my dreams.
>
> *Margaret Moss Painter*

Thoughts on My Birthday

I'm feeling so much love from my family and friends. I couldn't make it without their support.

I went alone to get my biopsy results. It was lonely, sitting there all by myself in the doctor's examining room, waiting to find out if the biopsy results were negative. Rick was always by my side for all those scary things. The biopsy was negative, no evidence of hyperplasia, come back in a year.

No one to hug and kiss in celebration. God, how I miss his giant, hard, embrace.

I went to Marsha's for carryout breakfast. She had the boys in birthday hats and a sign on the wall.

Marsha also wrote a wonderful tribute to me on Facebook:

> Today is Gerry's Birthday! She has been so many things to me: Aunt, friend, confidant, mother. She has held my hand through the ups and downs of life and helped me laugh, cry, and worry myself through it all. This year I witnessed her go through terrible pain with a wisdom, strength, and sense of humor that had me in awe. Whenever I have to describe who she is to me to someone who doesn't know, I always feel like there aren't enough words to describe, like they'll never understand that she's not "just" my aunt. I have been so lucky to have her in my life. Happy Birthday!

The picture she posted of the two of us was horrible. Lol. I hate my pictures so much.

I feel the pain, and then I don't. I never know when it's going to hit. I want to get out and try to forget, but then I can't stand the idea of forgetting and want to be back in my cocoon, sitting cuddled up under the blanket you loved so much – your "special blanket," looking at your picture on the shelf across the room.

God I miss you.

November 22, 2017

Three Firsts

Rick has been gone three months. In the past two days, I made it through three firsts: I went to get biopsy results alone (uterine cancer scare), I celebrated my birthday, and, of course, Thanksgiving. I have so many things to be thankful for: the biopsy results were good, and my family and friends were supportive and wonderful on my birthday. My step-kids and their children came to Thanksgiving and there is no doubt that we are still family. Rick must have been delighted to see us all together yesterday.

And then they left. The door shut and I began to sob as if he had just died, and my heart felt like it was shattering all over again. I completely fell apart and spent hours just looking at pictures and crying, almost like the first horrible week after he died.

Today, I looked for the poem my friend sent me in the first week after Rick's death. I try to be upbeat and move on, but these lines describe how I feel perfectly. I will do my best to rebuild my life, and I will put on my positive front for the world, but deep inside, I will always always feel like this:

He was my North, my South, my East and West,
My working week and my Sunday rest
My noon, my midnight, my talk, my song;
I thought that love would last forever, I was wrong.

The stars are not wanted now; put out every one,
Pack up the moon and dismantle the sun.
Pour away the ocean and sweep up the wood;
For nothing now can ever come to any good.

"Funeral Blues" / "Stop All the Clocks" by WH Auden

November 24, 2017

Home Depot

Dear Rick,

How could I so easily forget the one place that has so much meaning, the place that would be so difficult to return to without you?

Home Depot was a huge part of our marriage. It started at your buddy Lester's, when we were planning to buy his house on land contract. We put a lot of work into that house and then walked away.

After buying the house in Maryland, we literally spent hours every weekend for another six years, roaming the aisles purchasing appliances, and parts, and lumber, and screws.

We tore our house back to the studs and rebuilt it by hand – which meant needing all sorts of tools, large and small – purchasing the smaller ones, renting the big ones. We'd start out Sunday mornings at Old Country Buffet for breakfast, then walk across the parking lot to the Home Depot.

You'd sometimes stop for things on the way home from work, but we usually shopped together on Saturdays and Sundays before taking on more hours of work on whatever project was currently underway. Then, after returning to Michigan, we started all over updating this house and we needed to make those same trips.

When your mom died, we spent how many years? At least three, doing it all over again.

Home Depot, and sometimes Lowes, was a major location for so much of our time together, building, rebuilding, updating our homes together. Watching out dreams come to fruition was wonderful and forged the deep connection, the bond we both enjoyed in our 21 years together.

So it's no wonder it hit hard yesterday when I went to Home Depot with Brandon and Jonas. For some fathomless reason, it never occurred to me that it would be difficult. I knew the diners where we had our breakfast every Sunday would be awful to visit without you, and going to movies without you, which was our weekly Thursday date – I knew that would sting. But Home Depot? How could I forget how much that could hurt, walking those hallowed halls without you?

It just seemed so wrong. I very rarely, if ever, went there to pick up anything without you by my side. It was always the two of us! I think I'm glad I was with Brandon the first time, and not alone. I'm not sure I could have even walked in the door by myself. I maintained my cool, but felt like sobbing.

Brandon left me for a few minutes while I entertained Jonas as he watched an employee, a forklift, and a garage door, and standing there with him, I had time for my mind to wander, and it started to hurt more and more. It was near the lumber – oh, how many times did we buy and look at lumber? Six or more decks, a front porch, fences…hasps and braces, latches and brackets.

God, I missed you then. I wished more than anything that we could have a do-over. I want to start from the beginning and enjoy the entire 21 years again, with you by my side, laughing, joking, arguing, swearing, but most of all just loving each other. Just being together day and night, week after week, month after month, year after year, decades with you by my side.

I can't stand this isolation. This is the greatest punishment I've ever endured.

Why? Why can't we have had more time together? I knew being married at forty meant we'd lost at least two decades we could have shared, but I hoped so much to live to be 80 with you. To retire and just be together, no matter how old, crotchety, lame, or sickly – I'd have loved my time with you.

I miss you, honey. I miss you and the life we shared. I miss weekends at the Home Depot and hanging out, and building our lives together.

November 26, 2017

The First Time I Felt Love

I was remembering the first time I really felt that he loved me as much as I loved him. He told me that, as he came home from somewhere and pulled up in front of our apartment, that when he saw my car, it made him happy. It made him excited to see me. He was glad I was home.

I had felt that feeling many times in my life when I was in an unrequited love. I certainly felt it many times when I saw Rick's car, or when I saw him waiting for me outside the airport as I picked him up when he came to town.

But until Rick told me that, until I heard those words, I had never had anyone else tell me that same thing. I had never felt that, yes, this person loves me as much – or even more – than I love him.

Those words were at the beginning of our relationship, when I was still in shock that Rick loved me as much as I loved him. He confirmed so much in so few words.

Over our 21 years together, he would continue to use his words, his action, and his touch to convey his love for me. But those words that came in the beginning spoke volumes about who he was and about how much love he held inside. His simple words made me feel really loved for the first time.

November 30, 2017

I Sit Here on a Cold Dark Evening Wondering How I Got Here

I sit here on a cold dark evening wondering how I got here.

How did I come to be a widow, sitting here alone in my quiet living room?

Where is my husband?
How did he disappear from my life so suddenly?

How can I so suddenly be alone with
no hopes
no dreams
no purpose

with my heart torn in two?

I know I can and should go on,
but I don't have any interest in the future.

I go to work
socialize
force myself to leave my bed every morning
shower
dress
leave my house
I eat my three square meals and feed my cat

But I'd rather not.

I'd rather stay in bed and hope I'll dream of him

curled up in his favorite blanket
crushing his pillow to my chest

I'd rather surround myself with pictures of
my love
my life
my past

I'd rather grab at any chance to relive our life together
in my mind

I talk to him
cry to him
and long for what will never be again

I accept that he's gone,
but no matter how much I attempt to amuse myself,
no matter how I try,

I'd rather be with him than left on this journey alone.

Half of me is gone

and the part that's left is empty

November 30, 2017

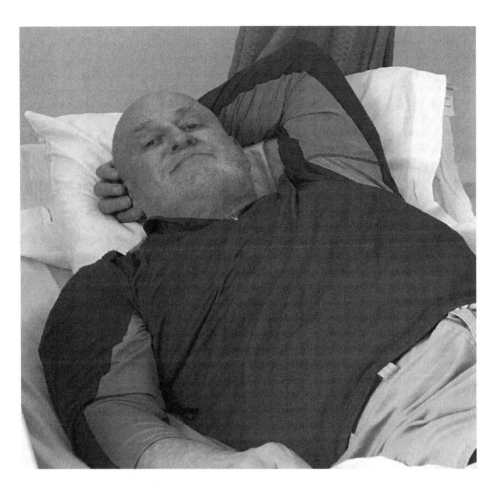

One More Time

Would one more time have helped?

I am once again swamped with regrets for the times I was too wrapped up in other activities (or my exhaustion or sadness and despair) to drop everything and come to you, join you as you lay in bed. But would one more time, one more embrace, one more talk have helped assuage this great engulfing grief?

You are gone. I lie here alone, facing the empty side of the bed where your huge muscular body should be. I reach for you in the night and awaken with longing for what will never be again.

Perhaps the few times I failed to join you, those missed moments would have left me with fewer regrets today, but the grief from your absence wouldn't be any less painful.

I think the real pain is in imagining that I hurt you when I put off your requests. Did I cause you one moment of sadness in your too-short life? That's what's painful to me now.

The idea that by denying you anything at all in those last months of your life means that I caused you pain or disappointment when you had so little left that made you happy, the thought that my failure to see how much you needed me and those times just lying in bed together causes me great pain and guilt.

The regret that I may have missed one more chance to hold you and love you, or that even worse – I hurt you – adds one more spike in my self-inflicted crown of thorns.

December 1, 2017

I Want to Be Alive Again

And I don't want a never-ending life
I just want to be alive while I'm here
The Strumbellas – Spirits

I'm still me.

I was a whole person before I met you and a whole person while we were together. I'm still that person.

I feel fortunate that I don't have the issues so many other widows have. I had a place of my own, a job of my own, independence, a full identity before we met. Now, I have all those things, and a better life from all that we built together, and all that you planned and left for me.

But...

I miss you. I know I have a life. I know I have a future. I know have people who love me. I have supportive friends and family.

But...

I don't have you.

I'm missing my greatest fan. My partner. My lover. My soulmate.

I don't want a never-ending life. But without you, I don't feel alive while I'm here.

December 2, 2017

The Ikea Furniture

Dear Rick,

Remember when we picked out the new living room furniture together? It was a little more than a year before you died. I took photos. The date on the pictures is May 22, 2016 – around 12:30 p.m.. We didn't even have a clue about what was ahead as we enjoyed ourselves on that happy day. We didn't know that in a few short months – in September – the medical nightmare would begin.

It was a Sunday and we were at Ikea. Remember all those trips to Ikea when we lived in Maryland? We so enjoyed going there, seeing the cool decorating ideas, the trendy furniture, the candles and stemware and baskets and art. You especially liked their big, big art prints. Unfortunately, we never had enough wall space in our small homes to hold all of the ones you liked.

You got your giant Reno print there. The one in your office. And the living room abstract art that used to fit so beautifully over the maple fireplace that we built in the family room in Maryland now hangs in our Michigan living room. The giant red poppy-like flower is still in our dining area.

Ikea and Home Depot played such a large part in our marriage. We were both thrilled when Ikea came to Canton. We loved going to that store. We dreamed up ideas at Ikea and then we created them with the tools and resources from Home Depot. I've been to both stores without you now. I sobbed for hours when I returned home from each venture.

But oh, the memories…wandering the aisles, planning our future, creating our perfect world, our safe haven, our love nest. Each home, each project, each day spent working with you to achieve our goals created such great memories, memories for me to cry over now.

Even the mid-project arguments are special to me. We came, we fought, we conquered – and we stayed together, in love for eternity.

Except it wasn't for eternity, was it?

Was it?

Are you here with me now?

I read a great quote on a post in my Facebook widows' group:

"The love is still there. You're just in different places."

I keep looking for signs of you, and thinking I'm seeing them. I long to be with you so much, to hear your giant laugh, to feel your massive arms around me, squeezing me too tightly. To match wits with you, to annoy you, to just be.

So today, on a Sunday in December, four months after your death, I look at pictures from the spring before our nightmare began, before your body betrayed you – and me. We didn't buy the furniture that day, because we wanted to think over our priorities. Did we want to spend a thousand dollars on furniture?, or another trip?, or a MacBook?, or…a million other things we wanted.

We didn't buy it once you were diagnosed, because we foresaw some hard living ahead. As the consummate planner, I made you bring up the two ugly recliners from the basement in advance of the chemo, and the puking, and worse. We agreed it wasn't a great time to buy new furniture.

After the chemo, when you went into remission in February of the next year, we decided the furniture still wasn't a priority; the trip to Florida was a much better investment – and oh, honey, it was! Then we got the bonus trip back, courtesy of Jo. Those six weeks we had together, you wandering around in the beautiful sunshiny weather by day (as you so loved to do), then coming home to the condo to nap in the next room, while I worked on my laptop – sometimes taking a break to join you in bed. Both of us spending each evening eating and drinking at outdoor venues, viewing the sunset every night on the beach, returning to the condo to cuddle up on the couch and watch TV – both trips were so awesome. You were so happy. We were so in love.

So, that's all gone now.

I'm alone in our world. It's a cold December day. No more sunshine in my life, no more cuddling, caressing, dreaming, sharing, laughing. I've decided I must buy the furniture – now, before it's too late, before Ikea discontinues it, and it slips through my fingers.

I'll finish that plan we began in May 2016, on that happy Sunday, one of many happy Sundays, and every time I sit on the sofa or loveseat, I'll know we picked it out together, and I'll feel you next to me just a little, one more time.

December 3, 2017

August 13 · Traverse City

tonight as i put jonas down i hummed a different tune not sure why foo fighters pop'd in my head but it did, and i just went with it. it was only moments before that i found out we lost a great man....a husband, a tall papa, a father, a friend... it's never easy loosing a loved one...but this one will be really hard. my boys lost a papa.

"It's times like these you learn to live again
It's times like these you give and give again
It's times like these you learn to love again
It's times like these time and time again"

Rick, we love you.

It's Times Like These

I was driving to my grief counseling session, foolish enough to listen to the radio.

I can't listen to music anymore, and music is something I've loved my whole life. Music is passion and feelings and emotion and more. A passionate love of music is also something Rick and I shared.

We had different tastes in music, but we both had such eclectic taste, so many likes and dislikes that there were whole genres of music that we mutually enjoyed.

He was a Paul Simon fan. I was not. When Simon was with Garfunkel, yes, but don't tell me 50 ways to leave my lover, or put diamonds on the souls of my shoes.

I was a rebellious teen in the 70s – 3 years younger than Rick. Although we both loved much of the music from the sixties and some early 70s, we branched off when it came to hard rock. Give me some Led Zeppelin or Black Sabbath. Rick wasn't interested.

He liked folk music. I could tolerate some of it.

I introduced him to Celtic and bagpipes. We eventually shared a love of Carrickfergus by Van Morrison and the Chieftains.

We agreed on classical – a thumbs up from both of us. In the past year, we discovered the Vitamin String Quartet – the group covers dozens of popular songs that Rick and I both enjoyed. It could probably be considered elevator music, but it became our go-to music of an evening.

Five for Fighting's Superman, Walking in Memphis, some Elvis tunes, old Beatles, and even Monkees hits were on our mutual playlists.

So, not only is it difficult to listen to our shared songs now (each one evoking memories of evenings by the fire, or under our gazebo, or on the beach, or in our quiet living room), there are even songs I never cared for very much that elicit strong feelings.

Rod Stewart sings, you're in my heart, you're in my soul…and tears begin to fall, although I'd never particularly cared for the song before.

If a song was popular during that last year together, whether we liked it or not, I feel the pain of that time again. "Unsteady" by the Ambassadors wrenches my heart strings from remembering how my strong, muscular husband weakened so much that I supported him as he walked (Hold, Hold on, Hold on to me, 'Cause I'm a little unsteady, a little unsteady… if you love me, don't let go).

Old songs or new, if they mention missing you, loving you, life without you, there will never be another you, or any other of those sentiments, I have to turn the dial.

And so, I have begun to listen to audio books. I took over Rick's Audible account and listen to novels, new ones I'm purchasing with his left over credits, as well as books he has in his history, so I can feel closer to him knowing he was listening to this same story not so long ago.

But today, I didn't connect my bluetooth Audible account to the radio. The ride to the counseling office isn't too far, so I took a chance on some music.

… It's times like these you learn to live again

I've never been a huge fan of the Foo Fighters, but as this song began to play, it spoke to me. I was on my way to grief counseling, for cripes' sake. Four months after my husband's death, I was trying to learn to live again.

But there was more. The song seemed so familiar, as if it was somehow significant, in some way related to Rick's death.

And then I remembered.

On the day Rick died, my daughter-in-law was stuck several miles away. My son made it to the hospital in time, but Lindsey stayed at the hotel room with their toddler and baby. That night, after putting one of my grandsons to bed, she wrote a beautiful post that included those lyrics.

tonight as i put jonas down i hummed a different tune not sure why foo fighters pop'd in my head but it did, and i just went with it. it was only moments before that i found out we lost a great man....a husband, a tall papa, a father, a friend... it's never easy losing a loved one...but this one will be really hard. my boys lost a papa.
"It's times like these you learn to live again...
Rick, we love you.

December 5, 2017

Katherine Gerry Billings Palmer added a new photo.
December 6, 2013 at 7:54pm · iOS · 🌐 ▼

Enjoying a balmy Michigan evening.

👍 Brenda Bradley, Brenda Williams and 10 others   3 Comments

Time Hop

Every morning I get a reminder from Time Hop…"see what happened on this date…"

I open the app with trepidation.

Will it make me laugh or cry? Will the photos from the past affect me like a dagger through the heart?

Four years ago…Rick sitting by the fire in the backyard. He's wearing his favorite red hoodie and the plaid jacket that I hastily grabbed from the front closet this morning when I took out the garbage. I've appropriated some of his clothing and jackets. I suppose it's an attempt to feel close to him again. He wore this. It touched him. He was alive.

How does today's photo make me feel?

Sad. Happy.

Sad that he's gone.

Happy that he was once here and part of my life…that we had those times by the fire, his favorite part of the day.

Grief for what will never be again.

December 6, 2017

The Little Losses

Now that I've been in mourning for more than 4 months, I think this grief thing is pretty predictable: I'll wake up each morning and immediately notice your absence. I'll either bury the thought and jump out of bed, or – on the weekends – I'll bury myself deeper under the covers and begin remembering you and our time together.

It's the little losses that are unpredictable.

I'm stressed at work, I want to turn to you to vent. You're not there.

I have a cold, I'm tired and cranky – you aren't there to cheer me up and bring me some comfort food. You don't feel my head with the back of your big, strong hand and make your pronouncement: no fever!

Nothing big. It's the little losses that pile up and eventually swallow me up in grief.

December 6, 2017

Sometimes I Wail

Sometimes I wail.

I don't just weep, or cry, or even sob.

I wail.

It's been a little more than four months since I became a widow. This is new territory for me. I met Rick when I was nearly 40, a never-married mother of one son. Marriage had eluded me. I'd obviously met men, since I was a mother, after all. But the idea of finding the man I'd want to spend my life with – that had proved to be impossible.

Oh, I'd come close. I met one man and fell deeply in love, despite the fact that on our first date he told me he'd be moving across the country. I was 20 and in love, so decided to bet the odds that just maybe he'd stay. In the end, despite his avowed love for me, he moved.

I waited for him to return. I could have followed, but I wanted proof that this was "the one." After all, knights in shining armor slayed dragons and traveled for years to be reunited with their fair maidens.

My knight found a new damsel and married her.

My son's father? A nice guy, a guy who loved me. Not a guy I wanted to spend the rest of my life with, so we parted. He, too, moved across the country and married someone else.

There were others, the ones who wanted me but didn't hold my interest. And there were the ones I so desperately wanted to want me. As Grandma said, they wanted an apple, and I'm an orange. Try as I might, I couldn't become that apple.

So, as year 40 approached, I was surprised to find a man who not only wanted an orange, he loved oranges – big, round, juicy oranges. As luck would have it – finally! – he fit my 10-point list of what I wanted, too. He was big and muscular, check, check. He was extremely intelligent, check. He was kind and loving, funny and clever, read books, even wrote extremely well, check, check, check, check, check, check.

And, number 10 – he loved me.

So, at 40 years old, I marched down that aisle, wearing a white wedding gown (the nerve!) and had that dream wedding, marrying the man I had waited for: my soulmate, my friend, my lover.

We spent twenty more years in love, the newlywed kind of love, honeymoon love. After twenty years, we still held hands, enjoyed impromptu dances in the kitchen, met each evening on our deck to drink wine and talk about life, love, hopes, dreams. We spent long weekend afternoons lying in bed, listening to the rain, cuddling, laughing, wrestling, and spilling out all the secrets we could share only with each other.

We did everything together: trips, and chores, and errands. We renovated three houses – by hand – together. We traveled across country – loving our car trips because it gave us more time to just be together, exploring new places, doing new things. We were anxiously anticipating those golden years, when I could retire and we could spend more time on beaches, when we'd drive across the few states we missed, and then return to Europe where we'd finish the trip we began a few years ago.

And now he's dead.

He was diagnosed with small cell lung cancer in the autumn of last year. He made it through the chemo, lung and brain radiation, shots, transfusions, low white blood cell counts, low platelet counts, and every other horrific thing that comes with the treatment. In February, they told us he was in remission. We spent six weeks in Florida celebrating, swimming, watching the sunset each evening. We were on our last honeymoon and we lived it and loved and talked and cuddled and just were.

And then the complications began: the tiredness, the pain in his lung, the low sodium levels, the blood clots, the weight loss, the confusion ("Honey, I can't remember how to send a text message," said my tech-savvy, web designer husband).

Finally – even though the cancer was supposedly in remission, one of my bright ideas killed him.

Since he was starting to feel stronger and absolutely hated sitting around, I suggested he roll the empty garbage cans back to the house. He was excited to try something so mundane, yet "normal." He tried. He fell. He broke his hip. Fat embolisms from the femur break invaded his lungs.

Two days and four "code blue" resuscitation attempts later, I was a widow.

A wailing widow.

It all seems like a dream now. The 21 years we had together seem so long ago, yet like yesterday, hence the dreamy quality.

How can it have been so long since we were together, since that night before he died, when I held his hand through the hospital bed railing? When we talked about how all we needed was each other, and to be together? Traveling or doing other things, be damned. Who needs vacations or projects? We don't need anything but to hold hands and watch TV while he recuperated for the next six weeks from the hip surgery scheduled for that weekend. We'd just sit next to each other and talk and listen to music and love each other, and then he'd be fine and life would be normal again. After all, the cancer hadn't returned.

The best laid plans of mice and men...

Yesterday, I wrote an essay, a memoir, about the whole ordeal, from diagnosis to death. I wrote for six hours. I finished, closed my computer, and sat.

And then it began, like a huge rolling wave, up from my gut: the wail.

It started with one quiet tear running down my cheek, then two, then the sob, then grabbing my heart because it felt like it was literally rending in two. Then the sob began to get louder. It became nearly a roar – that's the best that I can describe it. A roar, a howl, pain that just couldn't be contained.

I have never been a wailer in my life. I am now. I think it's the only thing I can do.

It's winter, so the doors and windows are shut tight. I live alone, so only the cat can be startled. So, I will wail. I will wail until I have no more pain inside me.

I will wail for myself and all I have lost – so quickly, so unfairly. My love, my only love, is no more. He's relegated to photos and videos. He's my imaginary friend, the person I talk to as I sit alone in my cocooning chair – the place I have created to feel safe, now that my big, strong protector is gone.

Most nights, and many hours on my empty weekends, I cuddle up in my chair under his favorite blanket, often wearing his sweatshirt or socks, and I talk to him, doze and dream of him. I long for his arms around me, and I cry quietly for all that I've lost. It comforts me. It's how I grieve and experience and release the greatest pain I've ever known.

But sometimes, sometimes when it's too much, when I relive the hours before his death (the defibrillator paddles and my desperate begging for him to live), or I think of all the suffering he endured, or I grieve for some pleasure he will miss, or some way I failed him at the end (I'm so sorry I couldn't save you) – at those times, I wail, because it's all I can do to relieve the pain.

December 10, 2017

A Visit From You

The printer just made the cycling noise that lets me know you are here.

So I started blabbing to you. I think you may be around at other times, but when I hear this, I jump at the chance that you're trying to tell me you're here.

I love you. You know that.

I wonder what you think when you see me alone and crying, wailing.

I think of how that would affect me, watching over you and seeing you in your misery. I would hate it, of course, but what can I do? This is awful. This is miserable.

I try to go on. Some days, I think I can. I have more hope in a future on my own. I feel not quite excitement, but slight anticipation of an upcoming event – meeting my friend Tina for a movie/dinner night, the work Christmas party, things like that. I look forward to escaping my solitary tomb for a little while.

But then I long to come back home, to you, to your photos, and videos, and your "stuff."

I don't want to go on. I want to stay in our world, try to recreate it, memorialize it, feel it again in some small way by touching your things, watching our TV shows, but usually, staring at your picture and talking to you.

I don't want to leave you behind, but I know I must.

December 11, 2017

I Went to Costco Today

Dear Rick,

I went to Costco today.

I doubt I've ever gone without you. Maybe once, but maybe not. Costco was us, just as Home Depot, Lowe's, Ikea, and all those other stores were places we went together.

Roaming the aisles of Costco with you was one of life's simple pleasures, one of our "our world" things to do. You and I called each other across the aisles, "Rick, come see this kitchen item!" "Gerry, look at this gazebo!" "Hey, look, it's that blankety blank we've been looking for!"

Oh god, I miss you so much! I miss all the delightful, simple pleasures we shared.

I went to Costco, but forgot to take my Visa credit card. It's all they take now – has been for awhile. Since I was always with you, and you had yours, I didn't even think to grab it. So I went to optical to make an appointment. Remember, our insurance pays for an exam and a pair of glasses biannually and we were supposed to go earlier this year? But we couldn't. First, we were in Florida, then you were too sick or weak to walk those long aisles.

I remember you did go to Costco, one day, when I was at work earlier in the year. We were going to our friend Wally's and you bought appetizers. You bought some kind of sandwiches, which I thought were way too much as a prelude to a dinner, but everyone loved them and it made you happy. I liked when you were happy, pleased about something you had accomplished. You didn't get a lot of praise, and you deserved so much for all you did and were and strove to do. I tried my best to let you know how proud I was of you, of being your wife, of being by your side. I hope you knew. I think you did.

It still hurts so much, you not being here. Four months – I don't know how I've made it this long, missing you – not being able to touch you or hear you or see you. My imagination isn't quite strong enough to pretend that you're hugging me in bed at night. I've tried. I've closed my eyes and pictured it as vividly as I can, but it doesn't work. You aren't here – here where you should be.

So, today, alone, I went to Costco. I had my eye exam and tried on some frames. In 20+ years, I've never picked out glasses without you. Yup. It's the little losses, the ones you don't see coming. Going into a Costco without you, picking out frames without you, coming home to an empty house, eating dinner alone. It's a million thoughts and a million things everyday that all scream, WHERE IS HE? HE ALWAYS DID THIS THING WITH ME!

I want to talk to you about so many things. Tonight, I have to work on the newsletter you created, sitting at your desk, working on your computer, in your office. And I don't want to! I want you to do it! I want you to be here working on the newsletter, then stop for a break and put on your layers of sweatshirts, hoodies, flannel, and go out to have some wine on the deck. And I'll surprise you by coming out for two glasses. And you'll tell me all the thoughts that are mulling around in your head: your ideas, your decisions, your plans, your dreams. And I'll chime in and we'll discuss, and debate, and argue, and agree. And then I'll tell you I'm too cold, and I'll rise to go in and as I pass you, you'll grab my hand and pull me to you for your kiss. And you'll thank me for coming out and tell me it's the best part of your day, and then you'll pat my ass as I walk away, and I'll yelp at you.

I want that so bad.

I want the little things, life's little pleasures.

I want you.

xx

December 20, 2017
18 weeks

You Died When I Left the Room

This morning I woke up, and foolishly went to the widows' support group on Facebook. A woman mentioned the theory that our loved ones wait until we leave to die. They hold on until that time, then you may go to get a drink of water, take a bathroom break, and that's the time that they die.

I immediately thought of you dying. The code blue, the paddles. I had left your room and was making a phone call. It had only just occurred to me (with a vengeance) that you were possibly going to die.

It's odd, because I felt it. I felt it the night before when I left to go home and get some sleep. How often did I stay, sleeping in a chair overnight, just to keep you safe? But, no, the nurse came in for the night shift, they told me you had spiked a fever, you were uncomfortable, and I kissed you and left.

I don't know what I was thinking. Was it was sort of a self-preservation thing? I remember thinking that I needed sleep because the next day was going to be a tough one.

I cried a lot that night. I texted you, even though I knew there would be no response. You were sedated and intubated and wouldn't see the texts, but I had to pretend that there was a connection between us – as there had been nearly continuously since the night we met.

So I texted you at bedtime, then texted you when I woke up. I told you I was coming. You were oblivious. You were sedated and intubated, so there was no way I could actually get through to you. But I thought you'd get my message – telepathically – that our bond was so strong, you'd hear me somehow. I think you did.

I was overwhelmed with a premonition – a vague, unnamed feeling in my gut that this "wasn't going to be a good day."

Yet, still, as I sat by your bedside that morning, as the doctors continued to stream in with bad report after bad report, it still didn't really sink in that you were going to die.

At one odd moment, I glanced toward the calendar, and then thought, NO. I don't want to see the date. I don't want to make this date significant. As if ignoring the number would mean you would live. As if ignoring the number meant I wouldn't have it etched in my memory forever: August 13, 2017, the day my beloved died.

December 21, 2017

Christmas

They talk of Christmas, but to me it's just another day without you.

It's just another day that you're gone.

December 23, 2017

New York Times 2017 "The Lives They Loved"

In 2012, after my father died, I submitted his story to the NYT's The Lives They Loved section. For some reason, it made me feel better – my father was a simple man, no movie star or world leader, yet he was bigger than life in my world. Publishing his story in the Times seemed right. It proved he was important enough to be memorialized and have his story known and read by others across the globe.

At the time, I never dreamt that I'd be writing Rick's story so soon.

I was invited by several people to join them tonight, New Year's Eve, but I declined. I love them and thank them for loving me and for trying to help me through this grief journey, but I wanted to be alone tonight – alone with my memories. I believe leaving 2017 behind is one of the most difficult things I've encountered. I'm not sure exactly why. I know I'll never forget Rick, but I fear leaving this year – and him – behind. He was IN this year. He lived it. He existed. He will never see 2018 and I will go on without him.

I realized tonight that I've never been alone on New Year's Eve. I've had parents, my son, my family, or friends nearby for the last 60 years. Tonight, I will be alone with my memories and my love. Tonight, I will write of the Life I Loved and submit it to the New York Times. I've cleared a path in the snow and I'll sit under Rick's gazebo, wearing his hoodie and drinking wine by his fire.

Tomorrow, I'll continue trying to live without him.

Here's the story of Rick, in 400 words or less, as submitted to the New York Times.

> In March 1996, I met Rick Palmer in an AOL chat room. A year later, we married and, for the next twenty years, he took me on the ride of my life.
>
> We downed shots in Tijuana, sipped wine in Boston's Palm Restaurant, swam at a nude beach in California, and ate lobster in Maine. We gathered beads on Bourbon Street and talked politics at DC

parties. We toured Amsterdam's red light district and my ancestors' Cornwall village. We gambled in Vegas, visited the Grand Canyon and drove Highway 1 from Maine to Florida. The consummate wanderer, Rick never liked to plan ahead. 'Let's see what we find,' he'd say.

Rick played guitar, and sang with a deep husky voice that earned him awards at Karaoke contests across the US. His rendition of Garth Brooks' 'The Dance' earned him my heart.

Rick was a self-made man. He earned a football scholarship to WMU but dropped out after his father died, and built a career by initiative and hard work. He began as a baggage handler at an international airline and was promoted to ramp supervisor. He volunteered to write the local union publication, moved to the district level, earned more than 30 awards, and was invited to the international office. In 2011, he took an early retirement to dedicate himself to our web and print design business.

A tireless worker, Rick renovated three homes. He was passionate about music, photography, Stan Lee comics, and cooking. He was an avowed liberal and a voracious reader who avidly consumed the daily NY Times and several books each month. He was a wordsmith, an excellent writer, and a dreamer who loved the sound of thunderstorms and distant train whistles outside our bedroom window.

Rick loved his hometown Garden City, Michigan, and volunteered his design skills to community organizations. He rode his bicycle more than 10 miles a day, listening to his latest book. He fancied himself an 'old curmudgeon,' yet he made friends wherever we went.

Rick gave me 21 unforgettable years of love, laughter, and adventure. His life was cut short by cancer, but he sure lived in the time he had! Rick had a huge heart and an indomitable spirit. He was my husband, best friend, travel companion, business partner, writing coach, and champion. I found Rick Palmer in an AOL chatroom, and my life was never the same.

December 31, 2017

Would You Still Be Here?

I wake up every morning with some depressing thought.

Sometimes it's picturing you the day you died. Sometimes it's remembering how your mind was starting to go in those last months.

Of course, I never know what it will be. I only know it will cause pain, and then I'll put it away and go on with my day. Some thoughts I've been through dozens of times, and I have my pat answers ready – those are the easy ones. Some thoughts are worse. They seem to cling to my mind no matter how many times I've gone over them. How many times I've told myself to stop with the guilt. It's over. He's gone. I did my best.

I thought I was done thinking about today's question. I thought I had put this one to rest, but apparently there is no "done" when it comes to grief. My counselor said it's two steps forward, one step back.

The thought of today: If I had done something different, would you still be here?

If I had insisted on a different doctor, or set of doctors, or hospital? If I had asked more questions? If I had done something that day when you were dying, insisted on more answers?

Is there a way that you could still be here, healthy, in remission, if I had done something to change the outcome?

Was I too passive?

Did I miss something I should've seen?

We'll never know, will we?

January 6, 2018

What If?

It's going on five months now
I thought the "what-ifs" were over

I thought I had locked them away in a box after examining every single one
carefully
minutely
looking them over and over

and castigating myself for what I could have done.

But apparently it's not over
Apparently someone unlocked the box

Perhaps I should've hidden the key.

The Pandora's box is open again and the
what if's
and the regrets
and the questions
and the guilt
and the self-recriminations
and all those other horrifying feelings

are rushing into my brain.

How did the box open again?

I thought we were done with this.

January 6, 2018

Picking at the Scab

At my grief counseling appointment last week, I expressed to my therapist, Vaiva, that — as I start to feel more "myself," stop thinking about Rick continuously as I had for the first few months — I'm more afraid of the pain that I know will come when I do think of him again. She said, it's analogous to picking at a scab that's beginning to heal. The pain from the wound isn't as great now as it used to be, but, as the scab tears again, it causes fresh pain from the wound all over again.

Today, as I returned from breakfast alone, missing him more than ever, and feeling my heart break again at the thought of a future without him, I realized the truth of the analogy.

I had major surgery August 13, 2017. My husband was surgically removed from my life.

Do I even compare him with a cancerous organ? That seems a vicious analogy, but actually, the healthy vibrant "real Rick" was changing. He was sick and weak and rarely laughed out loud anymore. I was reading an old email I found among the papers he had saved. He had printed and filed an email I sent him from early in our relationship. I met him in March 1996 and the email was from May. Apparently, he had expressed his love for me and hadn't felt that I reciprocated. In my email to him, I told him how much – and what – I loved about him. I even included two poems. Right from the beginning, Rick was effusive with his words of love, but that had never come naturally to me, so I told him in writing all the strong feelings of love I was unable to express, and he kept the email.

In my writing, I included all the things I love(d) about him. I said that one of the traits I found so endearing about him was his enthusiasm for life. By the time of the "surgical removal" of Rick from my life, that enthusiasm was nearly gone. It had been worn away by all that he had suffered.

His extremely intelligent mind (another of the things that I loved) was still there, but he'd had lapses of confusion and distorted thinking – perhaps from the preventative brain radiation, or the effects of chemo brain, or maybe caused by the lower sodium levels – who knows? I only know that his mental state was one of the most difficult things I encountered in the ten-month ordeal.

I lost my father to Alzheimer's, and now those scary episodes were being relived with Rick. I could handle the physical traumas "we" both endured. It was difficult, of course, but nothing like going on a dinner date and having Rick ask me to buy him dancing slippers that he promised he wouldn't use when working in construction. Or ask me how to send a text message. Or ask if there was a correlation between what we were watching on TV and the effect of his pain medication. Did I think it didn't work if he was watching something violent on TV opposed to a nice show?

Those were the worst of times. Watching his muscles dissipate as he lost weight, was horrible. His thick, sinewy calves became nonexistent. Yes, that was horrible, but watching him lose his mind was the most awful thing I experienced, and knowing he was aware of it was truly horrifying.

So, back to the analogy. The Rick I knew and loved was fading, physically, emotionally, and mentally. He was being completely eroded by the effects of cancer and its treatment, until, finally, he was ripped from my heart and soul – the surgical procedure.

At first, the painful loss of this vital "organ" and the accompanying wound left me in a mental fog, my mind's natural way to cope. I stayed in that fog for the first few weeks, possibly the first few months. As the pain lessened from the minute by minute "contractions," (my niece's apt phrase) to hourly pangs instead, I began to be able to function in the real world. I went back to work, I went out to social events, yet the pain was always looming. I thought about Rick and longed for him constantly – Where is he? Wasn't he still here, in another room? What would he think of something I just experienced? How had I failed him? Would I really never touch him again, or feel his warm, strong embrace?

I often needed to return home to freshly bandage the wound – as best I could, then curl up in a ball and sob through the continued ache of his loss.

Now, at nearly five months, I'm aware that the fog seems to have nearly lifted, at least I think it has. How often are we not aware of our real condition until we look back and compare it to how we feel now? But, at the least, the pain can be managed. I can function more like my "pre-surgery" self. Most of the time.

But then there are the complications that can come after surgery, and something rips open the wound: a photo of him, seeing his clothing, walking into his office, a waitress I haven't seen in months at our regular diner who asks, "Is your husband coming?"

I'm digitizing old video tapes, attempting to gather every possible photo and memory of the time we had together. As the videos are being re-recorded, I start up the process, click play on the camera, click record on the computer, and leave the room.

But sometimes, I stay, although I know myself, and I know it's too early to handle some of these memories. Sometimes, I can't help but watch him as he demolishes our old house to ready it for the remodel. I see him flex his huge biceps and easily tear out huge pieces of lumber as if they were paper. I see again the "old Rick" and how vital and strong and full of life he was.

Or I watch a trip I recorded – he scoffed when I kept the tape rolling on our long driving trips across country – but those tapes documented our banter, our real-life conversations, us, as we once were.

Of course, I'll cry softly through the short scenes I've dared to glimpse, but one tape I happened upon had a different effect, a rare response that gives me hope that in the future, I may be able to enjoy the memories and find them less painful. I laughed out loud as I watched a scene from 15 years ago. I was recording as I ran backwards down the hallway, as he tried to grab me, tickle me, get even with me for admitting that I had hung his new abstract art print upside down two weeks earlier and he hadn't noticed.

I felt absolute joy at seeing my vibrant, fun-loving husband, chasing me – in his underwear. He was laughing his deep throaty laugh and I was giggling as I tried to elude him, then the tape stopped suddenly. Apparently, that's when he caught me.

But, more often than not, as I watch the memories unfold, I'll come to terms, yet again, with the fact that this is it. He is not coming back, ever, and all I have are memories. The wound spasms afresh and is nearly as bad as the day of surgery. I know I'm healing, but this scar will linger for a long time.

January 7, 2018

Love Is Not All

When we were dating, Rick and I went through our "poetry phase."

I was a recent U of M grad – an English major who surrounded myself with books of poetry throughout the house. Rick enjoyed most of the poems I recited to him – at least I thought he did.

Rick lived in Minnesota and I in Michigan and he flew home every weekend. He also travelled quite a bit for his job.

One night – I believe he was returning on a red-eye flight from California – he stayed up all night and greeted me at the airport the next morning excited to tell me what he'd done.

He'd memorized one of my favorite poems.

Love is not all: it is not meat nor drink
Nor slumber nor a roof against the rain;
Nor yet a floating spar to men that sink
And rise and sink and rise and sink again;

Love can not fill the thickened lung with breath,
Nor clean the blood, nor set the fractured bone;
Yet many a man is making friends with death
Even as I speak, for lack of love alone.

It well may be that in a difficult hour,
Pinned down by pain and moaning for release,
Or nagged by want past resolution's power,
I might be driven to sell your love for peace,
Or trade the memory of this night for food.

It well may be. I do not think I would.

by Edna St. Vincent Millay

January 10, 2018

The New Year

The new year always signifies a fresh start. What wonderful things will I experience this year? What new things will I attempt? What new hopes and dreams can come to fruition? Will it be a good year?

No, not this year.

This year signifies a new start, but not the kind I ever dreamed of nor wanted. This year is the first, in more than twenty years, that I will endure without my husband.

It actually can be taken farther than that. My son turns 37 this year. That means that this year is the first in 37 years that I enter the new year totally alone.

I was my parents' child, I was the single mother of my son, I was the wife of Richard Palmer. Now I am just me.

I dare to hope that I will have a fulfilling life ahead. I dare to dream that the pain of losing my beloved husband will diminish. I hear a tiny voice inside me saying, "you will be okay."

My logical side says that's a lie.

January 10, 2018

In Memoriam.

I keep making decisions in memory of Rick. He would have liked this or that. He and I picked out this furniture so I will buy it in his memory.

I just thought about the gazebo outside. There was freezing rain this morning and it's snowing now. I'll need to go out and clean off the canvas so it doesn't cave in under the weight of the snow.

Most people take down the canvas when winter comes. Rick never did, because rain, sleet, or snow, summer heat or frigid winter temps, he sat out underneath it every evening.

We've always kept our summer furniture underneath the gazebo all winter long. Each evening, Rick put on layers of hoodies and flannel and took a bottle of wine out with him to contemplate life. He was excited when we found and bought a propane "fire pit" that was easy to light and kept us both warm on our evenings out in the Michigan winter.

Of course, I only stayed out for minutes, maybe a half hour at the most. I hate the cold, and I only sat out because I loved that part of our day. So, I braved the frigid temps for as long as I could stand it (and the propane heater DID help). Then, when I could no longer bear it, I rose and said, "well, I proved my love again tonight." And Rick agreed that I had, and he thanked me and said he loved me and that he'd only be another couple of minutes – which could be true or not, depending on the night.

So, the gazebo stands, canvas still atop it as the snow comes down. I doubt I'll sit under it alone much this winter. I did go out and toast the new year in memory of Rick on New Year's Eve. It was literally about 4 degrees – we'd had a cold spell. I lasted only as long as the bit of propane that was left in the tank: about a half hour or 45 minutes.

And now the propane tank needs refilling. I may do it. I may get a new tank and sit outside a few nights this January or February, just to literally "chill" at the end of a long day at work.

But really, I think about just taking down the canvas until spring. The thought occurred to me that Rick always wanted a strong, metal gazebo like he saw at Costco one year – I thought perhaps I'll get it – in memory of him. And then I question what that even means.

He isn't here to enjoy any of the things I contemplate purchasing. He's gone, he's absent from real life, so how would my purchase of something he used to enjoy when he was alive or would have enjoyed if he was still here help him in any way?

Do I think he's watching and smiling and saying, thanks Ger. Thanks for buying that for me; I'll enjoy it in my spirit energy world?

He's beyond things now. He'll never use anything again. At least I assume that's how it works. He no longer has the material body, so of what use is any material substance?

So why do I do it? Why do I consider buying things for myself based on if he would've used them if he was still here? Or do things in his memory? Because I'm trying to hang onto him. I try to hang on to anything he liked or would have liked. I don't want to give up one scrap of his existence. I don't want to relinquish what we had, what we planned, or what we could have done.

I don't want to give up any part of him.

January 12, 2018

I Woke Up Feeling Good Today

Tomorrow is the five-month anniversary of your death.

Five months.

I couldn't have imagined living five months without your touch, without seeing your smiling face, hearing your throaty laugh.

Five months without your witty repartee – and lame jokes.

Five months without your love.

However, for some unfathomable reason, I feel good, like I may have a future.

This is the oddest sensation, and one I haven't felt for much longer than five months. After the diagnosis, in the final 10 months of your life, I endured nearly constant stress, anxiety, fear that you'd be gone soon – an absolute devastating mind-numbing fear of surviving the rest of my life without you to wake up to.

How could I live without you? How?

Well, I did. I had no choice.

I woke up, and I got out of bed – every day.

I woke up, I dressed, I worked, I ate, I forced myself to live another day, every day.

It really kind of bothered me when people said I was strong. Why would they say that? I didn't feel strong. I felt like a complete and total baby, trying to live when I didn't have a clue how I would survive the unsurvivable loss of you.

So, I politely accepted the compliments. But never believed them to be true.

Then last night, it hit me. I really AM strong.

It really took all the guts I had to get out of bed every single morning since the day you left me. I didn't want to. I didn't want to live, let alone get out of bed, shower, and go about these horrible dreadful days. To know that hour upon hour I would feel such pain. To know that every single fucking day I would feel so awful that I didn't want to even imagine how the next day would feel.

It almost became worse as the fog lifted a bit. Like the anesthesia was being slowly removed and the sharpness of the pain would hit even more. The numbness wore off, and thankfully, the pain was no longer constant, but it was that much more painful each time it returned. It returned with a vengeance.

Each time I had a respite from the pain, I knew it would be short-lived… the few hours at work when it hit me that I didn't think of you constantly, waiting for your text, or thinking for a minute that you'd be outside waiting to pick me up for lunch. The nights when I could actually distract myself from longing for you to be here with me, when I sat home, alone, without you to talk to, yet content for a few minutes, or even hours, just playing on my laptop, or watching some inane TV show.

Those tiny gloriously pain-free moments frightened me because I thought, maybe now, maybe now I will be able to enjoy my life again, just a little. They frightened me because I knew from experience that within minutes, something would trigger a memory and I'd be a puddle on the floor, once again.

So, maybe today is different, but maybe it's just my vain hope that I will be able to live again without you, to actually feel joy again despite having to navigate the rest of my life without my partner, my love, my Rick. At least, today, this minute, I feel some semblance of hope.

It's an odd sensation. It's all I have right now, so let me enjoy it while I can.

January 12, 2018

I Don't Know Where He Is

I don't know where he is.

All religions have their explicit, concise answers for where the spirit goes after leaving the body. Heaven, limbo, another realm.

But no one really knows.

Those who write those "life after death" stories, describe the light, walking down a path, a glorious, peaceful feeling. They see long-dead relatives, they are filled with grief when forced to come back to life and earth.

Scientists debunk this ideal vision by saying it's some chemical thing, some giant burst of endorphins that flood the body as a coping mechanism at death.

So who really knows?

I choose to believe that Rick is sitting on the beach, right at the water's edge. He's in his favorite folding chair (the one with the fold down side table). He has a bottle of wine and he's waiting for the sunset. The actual photos and videos I have of him waving to me are on Lake Huron, so that helps me envision him at that location, but our many glorious photos and videos from our last trip when he was healthy and happy last year were recorded on the gulf in Florida.

No matter the location, there's sand and sun. There's peace and happiness and hope and love. And he's feeling no pain. There's no cancer. He feels only contentment as he sits across from an empty chair and waits, waits for me to join him.

In the video that gave me this wonderfully hopeful vision, I'm walking toward him, recording, and he looks up at me and waves. He's looking forward to me sitting across from him, anticipating us toasting the day and spending the next hours talking over events and plans and hopes and dreams.

He's waiting for me to join him. And, God, I want to. I can't wait to be with him on that beach for eternity. I'll tell him how much I missed him, how difficult it was to go on without him. I'll describe all the good things he missed, things he would have enjoyed so much – I'll describe them in detail so he can relive them vicariously through me.

Of course, that's if he's not here watching me now.

If he is here, if he's this presence I feel sometimes in the room, and the feeling that he's always inside my heart, then we'll rehash all those events and I'll get to hear his views, from his "heavenly" perspective.

But mostly, I'll just drink him in, feel the perfect wholeness at being reunited with my soulmate. I'll be complete once again.

That's my vision of heaven.

January 13, 2018

You and I Were a Team

Dear Rick,

I had my performance review today. I always called you immediately after talking to Sam and told you what she said. You always told me you were proud of me, and of course, excited when there was any possibility of me getting a raise in my future and our circumstances improving as they have been in the past few years.

I always had you there rooting me on. I miss that. Of course, you know I have family and friends who are there for me, but you were different. You and I were a team. You and I were one.

I want to call you now and tell you everything that's happening. I want to hear your encouragement, your advice, and your ideas. I want the closeness that we had.

I'm trying to find a substitute for each void that's in my life now. I can work and drive and cook and take out the garbage. I have groceries delivered! (LOL – You would hate that!) I have friends to go to movies with me. I'm back on the trivia team without you.

I can do this. I can be a solo act again. But most of all, I miss the connectedness I had with you. I miss my other half.

I love you.

January 17, 2018

If I Don't Grieve You As Hard, Does That Negate Our Love?

Dear Rick,

It's Friday. I'm working at home.

It just occurred to me that the pain isn't as great anymore. That continuous ache in my heart hasn't plagued me this morning.

Maybe I don't want it to go away. The ache of missing you is somehow what I owe you. I loved you (LOVE you) so much, that it's what I owe you. To hurt, to feel the pain of your loss.

It's an odd thought. If I don't grieve you as hard, does that negate our love? Is that the cockeyed thinking that's been somehow under the surface nagging at me as I start to heal?

I know that in an instant I can see your face again and feel all the old pain resurface. One word that reminds me of you, one stray thought, one random occurrence can bring back all the pain of losing you. So why can't I accept and rejoice in the fact that I HAVEN'T felt that yet this morning?

You were in parts of my dreams last night, and I awoke with a dull ache and a longing for your death to be a figment of my imagination. But I didn't feel that all out, wailing, screaming, horrific pain that I experienced so often: the mind-numbing, paralyzing kind, the kind that made me wonder if I could even go on living.

In the beginning, I had this vague fear that I wouldn't be able to go on living with so much awful and continuous pain. It was too difficult to contemplate more than one day ahead, sometimes one hour ahead, it hurt so terribly to be without you. A part of me was gone and I could see nothing but the pain of my loss – a loss of hopes, dreams, and happiness.

Oh, I never really planned to do myself in. I knew I wanted to live – and, when thinking logically, I knew I had a lot to live for: to be with those

I love, to try to rediscover things I desired, hopes for my own future. I knew logically that time would heal me, that I would feel joy again. After all, my parents, grandparents, and aunts are dead, and I rarely feel the pain of their loss anymore.

But maybe, deep inside, that's what I fear – that I will lose the connection I feel to you. While the pain is in evidence, you are still a part of me. You've been physically ripped from my life, but your spirit remains in my heart. The pain is just what I must suffer to keep you there.

And now, as the months go on, each day it hurts a little less, and the fog lifts a little more. I see some daylight. I forget to think about you. Being 100 percent consumed by grief has lessened to maybe just the horrible nights when I can't sleep from the pain, or to experiencing something you were so much a part of without you by my side.

Most days, it's a dull ache. It throbs sometimes, with perhaps an hour or two of sobbing, but the contractions have subsided and are no longer constant. I'm beginning to feel whole again, and I honestly think that scares me. Because it proves I can live without you. Is that insane? It just seems wrong, because I love you so much and long for you so much and NEED you to be here with me. I'm a confused mess.

January 19, 2018

The Weekend

Dear Rick,

I thought I was getting better, but I didn't make it through the weekend. Somehow I went from Friday feeling positive, feeling like I could go on without you, to Sunday evening, sitting in front of your computer, watching videos of us dancing at our wedding while I dissolved into a puddle of tears.

I guess I should've seen it coming. I've had those feelings of positivity before and they always end eventually.

Saturday was pretty good. I spent the day keeping busy. I had a little setback when I was doing taxes. Yes, I was doing taxes in January! I wanted to see how much we owe for last year, how much to budget for next year. I wanted to see how much we spent on deductions for the business and decide if I should keep going with it at all. So I did taxes, and that meant going back through the credit card records looking for deductions.

I followed our expenses all the way back to the beginning of last year. It was a little sad when I got to August and I saw the money I had spent for your obituary in the Free Press. I don't regret spending nearly $1000, because you were worth it. But it reminded me of all the decisions I had to make right after you died, and how awful it all was and the great fog that consumed my brain.

But then as I kept going backwards through July, June, May, April, I saw all the things we had done together: the diners, the movies and date nights nearly every week, a couple of doctor bills, just regular stuff. April was the worst. That was the month in Florida. It was our last happy month.

I saw the price of the Madeira Beach parking nearly every night and immediately thought of us sitting together, watching the sunset, me wondering if you'd be here next year and dreading the idea that – deep down – I didn't think you would be.

There were sunsets, there were restaurants, pizza places, just stuff. Just hanging out. There were the motels we stayed at. There were the Jack-in-the-Box tacos we ate coming and going when we stopped in Tennessee. And it brought it all back again. How wonderful and awful that trip was. It was a honeymoon that I knew was the end.

So I finished the taxes, picked myself up, and went to play with our grandchildren. I had a wonderful dinner with Brandon and Lindsay and her brother Mark, and I hung out with the kids and talked and laughed. Then I came home and, surprisingly, I was still OK and I thought yeah I'm getting better. It comes and goes, but it's not as bad as it used to be.

So I guess it's no wonder that Sunday morning I woke up missing you. I felt lost for a while. Should I go to a diner? Should I get up, dress, shower, go to a diner alone? No, I can go out later. I decided to stay home and relax, make a nice breakfast, and do my NYT crossword in this very quiet, quiet, quiet, quiet house. Sometimes I do our little routine, even though you're not here to do the answer part. Remember on weekend mornings, before I got out of bed, I'd yell to you in your office in the next room and you'd answer? It would be the same question and answer every time. So Sunday, I called out, "what are you doing?" And then I did your part too, and I called back, "waiting for you." And I chuckled to myself instead of crying.

So, yes, I thought, Wow! I'm really doing much better now. I had my breakfast, and I watched a recording of Saturday Night Live, just like we often did on Sunday morning. I talked to you during SNL in the parts I knew you'd especially like. I know you would've loved the part where Kate McKinnon played Robert Mueller. Just the bizarreness of her taking on that character. She was always your favorite, and I turned to your picture and said what you would have said to me: "Look honey, there's our Kate," Just like you would've said it, too.

It's really bittersweet doing all these things without you. All the things we always did together. But I did it, and I didn't cry, well maybe a little.

And then I thought, I have to get out of here; I have to get out of the house. But first, I'll do some work on our web business – you know, the work you always did. So I worked on the newsletter that you should be doing. And I guess I wasn't aware that I just kept getting sadder. Until I decided that's it, I'm going to go to the movies, I'm going to go out, get dinner, and go to the movies. But anyone I thought of inviting to go with me just didn't feel right. No one felt right. Because no one is you.

And I finally decided… wait a minute, my counselor would tell me I need to schedule time for grieving, so I went into the bedroom and I curled up under the covers and I talked to you, and I cried, and I sobbed a while, and I wailed, and I cried, and I couldn't stop. Because I miss you so fucking much I can't stand it.

I felt it all again, the way I don't want to go on without you, the confused realization that you really aren't here, the dread, the awful dread, of going through day after day without you. So much for getting better, eh?

When I finally cried myself out, I decided to stay home. Made a little dinner. But before I ate it, I went to your computer to get some fonts that I needed in preparation for working more on the newsletter tomorrow. And there on the hard drive was a video labeled "our wedding, 12 July 1997." And fool that I am, I watched it.

I watched me getting ready that morning with the girls in my apartment, me happy, me being excited because I was about to be married to you. I watched us kissing at the altar after exchanging our vows. I watched us wandering outside with the bridesmaids and groomsmen to take pictures. And then I fast forwarded just a little just to see how long the film was, to see if it needed cropping so I could post it on YouTube or your website for the kids and our friends to see.

And suddenly, I stopped fast-forwarding, because there was the two of us dancing to our wedding song. We were dancing to "You Are So Beautiful," by Joe Cocker – the song you sang to me at Karaoke all the time. And I was stroking your arm and your head, and you were leaning in and nuzzling my neck. We were so in love.

Why didn't we get forty years? Why were the last 20 stolen from me? Why were two people so obviously in love separated by death too soon? How can one of us go on without the other?

Yes, I started out this weekend thinking I was getting better. I was wrong.

I love you.

January 21, 2018

Mask

What's new? How have you been coping? How are you?

I'm fine. [I wail. I scream. I'm lonely. I miss my husband. My heart has been ripped out of my chest. I can't sleep at night. My soulmate is gone.]

January 28, 2018

A Special Kind of Lonely

Grief brings a special kind of loneliness.

You want to go out, and you can call anyone, but none of them are the one you want to be with.

January 30, 2018

Farmington Road

Dear Rick,

So, here I am, feeling really proud of myself for handling my new normal. I'm not crying all day anymore. I'm functioning. I'm planning a future without you. I'm being me, again, not always "us."

I'm planning my bucket list. I'm finding substitutes to try to fill the role you played in my life. I have friends and family to fill my hours, to go to dinners, and movies, and chat with about events in my life.

It's not perfect. There are times, like the other night, after I had worked all day on our business, when I wanted to go to dinner, but couldn't think of anyone in my "friends and family arsenal" to call. I rejected every idea, until I realized, I didn't want anyone but you. So I went alone and read my book, while drinking a margarita at the Mexican restaurant where we used to celebrate the end of the work day together. I was lonely, but only lonely for you.

I've cut my Xanax in half now. I'm not as anxious as I was. Oh, I felt it a little the other evening. Friday after getting home from work, I had nothing planned, and a giant lump formed in my stomach: unbridled fear. I was shocked. I had nothing to be upset about! Why was I so anxious, filled with dread?

Because I couldn't imagine filling those empty hours without you by my side. Because I suddenly became overwhelmed again by the idea of continuing for however many days and weeks and months and years without my other half. I felt that "ripped in two" feeling that I lived with for the first few months after you died. It came as a shock, because I hadn't felt that in a while. I was beginning to feel whole, and then suddenly, I wasn't. The amputee feeling pain in the missing limb?

As bad as the pain is now, it's absolutely nothing compared to before. I feel whole quite often now. I have a routine that doesn't include you. I'm filling in gaps.

So I was a bit surprised at what happened while driving to work this morning. There was an accident on Merriman Road, so I detoured and went to Farmington, instead. I had driven a few feet when I realized I had never taken that route since you died. It was the route you always took, but I never liked driving that way, so I haven't now that I drive myself to work.

This was the route where there is a four-way intersection and every morning, every single morning, you made a big production about coaching the other drivers through the organized process of the four-way stop. Sometimes you were irritated at the drivers who didn't get it and missed their proper sequence in the orderly process. Sometimes you lauded drivers for handling it correctly. But always, always, you made loud vociferous comments for my entertainment.

It was our routine, you cajoling or praising the other drivers, and me complaining that you took that route in the first place. Just avoid it and the irritation, I'd tell you, and we'd continue our banter about you and your commentaries on the "correct" way drivers should behave, and how irritating that corner was, and blah blah blah. It was our routine, and I miss it, and you, and the irritation, and the bantering, up to and including, when I'd finally say something that made you reach over and pinch my inner thigh – and I'd yelp very loudly. And we'd both laugh.

So, I turned that corner, and it all came rushing back, and I sobbed. I drove the rest of the way to work in misery, uncontrollably sobbing and stunned by how vividly I could remember you, and how much fun we had, and what I missed about you, and I once again felt that abject fear that I can't go on without you in my life.

And then I arrived at work, and I dried my eyes. I reapplied my mascara (I keep a spare in the car for these occasions), and I went on with my day without you.

January 31, 2018

The Sadness is Back

The sadness is back.

Maybe it's because I'm trying too hard to make plans, to think to the future. Maybe I'm not ready to let go of the past.

This morning, everything seems to trigger a memory. I was getting used to going a few hours, or maybe even all day, without thinking of him, but the weekend was one giant step backwards.

It could be because I entered the essay about the cancer ordeal in the

Fish Short Memoir Contest. Maybe reading the history of his illness and death over and over while I fine tuned the writing during the weekend made it rise too close to the surface.

Maybe it's because I was reminded this morning that I need to use 55 hours of vacation by the end of March, and I can't think of anything I'd want to do without him.

Or because the Super Bowl was yesterday, and we often had a party with the kids, or at least made some special snacks for the event. We'd sit together while he watched the game and I read a book, but I'd pause so we could enjoy the commercials together.

Maybe it's because of all the hype about "This is Us," and the main character dying. Maybe it's because I weaned myself off the Xanax. Maybe maybe maybe.

Valentine's Day is next Wednesday. Great. I should be on my way to Florida with Rick. My heart just constricted, just a little, at the thought.

Whether there are other reasons, or the few I just thought about, the weekend was a bit more difficult than it has been lately. I had to take much more time out to grieve. I napped and sobbed for more than an hour yesterday afternoon. I cried myself to sleep Friday and Saturday night.

God, I miss him. I keep returning to that shocked feeling I first had after he died. Yesterday, he came to mind and felt stunned and that phrase came back to mind, "I can't do this. I can't live without him!"

But I have to and I will.

February 5, 2018

Chasing Cars

I'm still having a tough time with the grief "episodes." I was doing so well, and now I'm not.

I question what has triggered this…tomorrow it will be six months since the day Rick died. Valentine's Day is Wednesday. We weren't big on celebrating what Rick called the "Hallmark Holidays," but most years, we were on our way to Florida on or around that day. I also quit taking Xanax just over a week ago.

And then there's the decision about how to use up vacation days that need to be used by the end of March. I can't picture enjoying any vacation without Rick, and I can't stand the idea of going to our special place in Florida and revisiting all those places we loved and sunsets without him.

So, I keep plodding along, socializing and putting one foot in front of the other. I don't have much choice, do I?

Today, I cried at breakfast because I went to a diner I hadn't been to since we went together. Then I cried over a song on the radio on the way home from trivia finals. Then I cried for no reason at all, just feeling that same anxiety and fear that I felt when he first died – how can I go on without him? How can he be gone? I miss him and love him and want him back!

THIS CANNOT BE! HE CAN'T BE GONE!

I went out to dinner. When I leave the cat home alone, I leave Pandora radio playing on my Amazon Echo. I know it's dangerous to leave the music going when I get back home, because so many songs trigger so many memories, but I left it on while I washed dishes. And then I heard the song from Snow Patrol that always always makes me think back to the last months of his life, when he would sleep so much, sometimes nap most of the day. And then he'd awaken and call to me to come lay with him.

I know it's my crazy widow brain just wanting some connection with him, longing to hear from him and touch him, but I feel this song – with it's crazy lyrics – has some that he's using to talk to me now. We did lay there together and forget about the world. Oh God, I so long to do that again – just lay in his arms and just "be."

The last words of the song mean so much –

> All that I am
> All that I ever was
> Is here in your perfect eyes, they're all I can see

All that he ever was WAS in my eyes as we lay there together. I loved him utterly and completely and he knew that without a doubt as we lay in bed and he looked into my eyes. And now all that he is, all that he ever was is in my heart forever.

> If I just lay here
> Would you lie with me and just forget the world?

I don't know where or when I'll see him again – will I see him when I die? Will we spend eternity together? I'm confused about how it will be, but I'm also confused about now…how can he connect with me? How can I hear him? But, the truth is, nothing will change for us at all. He will stay here in my heart and my memory exactly as he was when he was alive. Nothing will change for us now. Our relationship, our love, our connection will be forever the same as it was in August 2017, before he was sedated and died and left me behind.

And the memories of being held in his arms in our bed on many a summer's afternoon, just being together, being one with him, forgetting the world around us, will be with me forever.

February 10, 2018

Chasing Cars, Written by Nathan Connolly, Gary Lightbody, Jonathan Quinn, Tom Simpson, Paul Wilson • Copyright © Universal Music Publishing Group

I'm Angry

I'm angry.

I'm angry at life. I'm angry that he was taken from me. I'm angry that I'm sitting here alone on a Sunday morning staring at his picture and wondering how to fill this day.

I'm angry that he won't be joining me at breakfast – our breakfast – our special time on a Sunday morning at the diner, sitting across from each other. He'd read the paper and tell me interesting tidbits, or read me the advice column he liked so much.

I'd do my NYT crossword and try to beat Bill Clinton's 20 minute record time.

We'd chat and laugh and converse with the waitresses. He'd ask for a to-go container so he wouldn't be tempted to eat the huge portion he'd been served – with onions in his hashbrowns, of course.

I'm angry that it's all over. I'm angry that life isn't fair, that when you find that perfect person, that soulmate, that fun and wonderfully witty and loving mate you've longed for since you were a teen, that death steals him away.
I'm angry that he's gone from my life forever, and it's so, so, so, so empty now here in this house and in my life.

I'm angry that I'm trying to plan a vacation without him, my travel companion, my life companion.

I'm angry that the doctors couldn't cure the cancer. I'm angry that science hasn't solved the riddle of a disease that takes so many husbands and parents and children. Yes, let's build a wall. Let's have a military parade. Let's waste money on politics and hubris and war, instead of using the money to heal and give hope and keep people alive.

Rick would find it amusing that my mind turned to politics and the inanity of Trump. I miss his political diatribes. I miss his fascinating (and slightly peculiar) mind. I miss his zany sense of humor.

I miss his love.

So I'm angry. I'm angry that he smoked for years. Yes, I'm angry at that, too. I'm angry that neither of us foresaw how those cigarettes that accompanied a glass of wine would snuff the life from him at 63. I'm angry that we ignored the warnings about the consequences of smoking, that we gambled and lost.

And now the anger has abated, once again, and I'm just sad, and I miss him, and there's nothing I can do about it.

I guess I'll go to breakfast alone.

February 11, 2018

Our Site Gallery

Today, I was reminded that oursitegallery.com is going to expire. That's the website we created to show clients works in progress. Rick stored lots of files there when he was working on menus, flyers, and other print media. He used it as a backup as well as a location for client files.

Last May, when the domain was about to expire, we discussed whether to keep it or not. Now that I look back on the time, we were starting to downsize the company. Rick was losing weight, the pneumonitis wasn't abating. He was in remission, but he was weak. We still had hope that he'd recover, but it was a daily battle for him just to rise from his bed and keep up with the monthly newsletter he did for a major client, and to keep current with updates for the clients who paid for those.

I remember saying that we should just let the domain expire. I guess I knew we wouldn't be taking on any new clients, so we wouldn't need it for them to preview Rick's new designs.

Then I realized that the site had more than just "old files": it is a history of Rick's work, his designs, and his ideas. I couldn't just let that be wiped out. By now, I hoped against hope that he would live, but always in the back of my mind was the nagging thought that he might not be here next year. Wouldn't I want a chronicle of his works, a piece of his creativity to remember him by?

So I told him that I'd need time to backup all the files and sort through what was important and what could be discarded. And I honestly wasn't up to the task in the midst of doing my own job, helping him with clients, and most of all, helping him survive the ordeal of medications and hospitalizations and day to day living with his weakening body.

So here it is time to renew the domain name or let it go. It's time to go through the site. The domain expires in 90 days, so I thought I'd get ahead of the task and download all the files today.

And as I pour through the contents, it's made me sad.

I'm sad for so many reasons. I'm sad for the loss of a man who had such talent, and I question did I tell him that enough? He had won more than 30 awards in his career for his creativity and talent, but how often did I tell him that he was special?

I'm also sad for each file that reminds me of a client who took advantage of his sincerity and desire to please – who asked for numerous free updates, or dismissed his work or took for granted the fact that he'd really done a fantastic job.

I feel very protective of him now. He was always so strong when he was alive. Well, everyone thought so. But he often was insecure and trying to please others and not convinced of his talent. And I resent anyone who treated him with less than the respect he deserved. I see the one client's website that he recreated in Flash – after teaching himself the very technical details needed to do so. He was self-taught and he knuckled down and created a site that was perfect. At the time, we were trying to establish the company, so we were charging ridiculously low prices for small business clients. He definitely did not get the money he deserved for the work he put into the site.

He was an extremely hard worker. He loved what he did, but he still worked hard to achieve everything we earned. Did I tell him that enough?

As I look through this archive of his projects, I wish he was here so I could hug him and tell him how proud I am of him and all he accomplished. I hope he knew. I hope he felt my pride. I hope I told him enough.

February 20, 2018

The Grief Is Lessening and That Scares Me

Dear Rick,

I don't feel the grief all the time anymore. In the beginning, it was like a giant fog, like a veil over my face and head, over my life.

I thought about you constantly. I couldn't stop. Everything was a memory. When I was alone, all I could do was immerse myself in the grief of the loss and the thoughts and the memories of you.

But it's different now. There are whole chunks of my life that you're not a part of. It makes me sad. Happy, but sad. I want my life to go on. I want to be able to live without you, and I'm working hard towards that goal: to have a life again. But the more I work through the memories, the more I live on without you, the farther away you are receding into my past.

I don't want to lose you. I almost want to hang onto the grief so I don't.

It's a double-edge sword: working to move on with my life, working to make a life for myself, yet knowing with every step that the memory of you becomes more elusive, that you begin to have less impact on my thoughts, that you become a man I used to love, no longer my ever-present love, my partner, my companion.

This morning, I picked up my grief meditation book and there, in today's message, was this exact thought. How often does that happen and I think it's a message from you?

The idea of the essay is that the grief of the loss and love we had is so bound up together that we are often afraid to let the grief go. But grief and love can be viewed as two sides of a coin. And soon, when the coin is flipped, the memory of the love will always be on the top.

"At first these two—the grief and the love—are so wedded to each other that we cannot separate them. We may cling to the grief in desperation so we will be sure not to lose the love.

Perhaps the grief and the love will always be wedded to each other to some degree, like two sides of a coin. But maybe after a while, when we flip the coin, it will almost always be the love that turns up on top."

from "Healing After Loss: Daily Meditations For Working Through Grief" by Martha W. Hickman

Publisher: William Morrow Paperbacks; 1 edition (December 1, 1994)

February 24, 2018

I Miss My Best Friend

Dear Rick,

I have missed so much about you since you've been gone. I miss your love. I miss your touch. I miss your intelligence and wit and quirky sense of humor. I miss your huge strong body, and your muscles and your hugs.

I miss your unequaled and nonjudgmental acceptance of all that I am – foibles and failings included.

You were my unfailing champion, my biggest fan.

You were the smartest man I knew, and so accomplished in so many ways. You were a gifted designer and a talented writer. I so enjoyed working with you on our business, despite our differences and arguments – I loved the challenge of you. You were no simpering fop. You knew what you wanted. You had opinions. You were socially aware. You were a renaissance man.

You were also my best friend.

Until now, I've been missing your love and your companionship as a husband, as a soulmate. I've been immersed in the sadness of being a widow, a woman whose mate has died.

But this evening, as I sit here alone, I realized that a huge huge part of what I'm mourning is the loss of my best friend.

I liked hanging out with you. I could confide anything and everything to you and trusted you beyond life itself. You were there for me, always.

And we had so much fun just being together, day in and day out, playing games, chatting, dancing, just being in the same room, or even just under the same roof – shouting back and forth to each other.

What are you doing? What do you want to do today? When's dinner? Where do you want to go?

I saw another Marvel movie without you today. This is the second one since you've been gone. You would have loved it. And later, you would have explained all the nuances I missed. Yes, honey, I did notice Stan Lee in his cameo, but I still need you to explain the history and about the vibranium and the ending with Bucky. You knew the details and the stories and you shared your knowledge with me after every movie.

I need my best friend back. My whole weekend is spent finding things to occupy myself with. I filled the time working on the newsletter you created. I'm getting used to doing it now. And I went to dueling pianos last night and I had a really good time. I laughed. I had fun. And then I cried myself to sleep because I wanted you there with me to enjoy it by my side. And I wanted you in bed with me when I got home. I wanted to cuddle up to you and talk about the evening and plan our Sunday.

I went to see the movie – Black Panther – with Brandon and Lindsey at 11am. It was the only time we could go with Sue watching the kids. And I wanted you there. But I filled the time, and kept occupied, and finished the newsletter. And here I am again, alone, and missing my best friend.

It was effortless filling the time with you by my side. Whether we had something to occupy us or not, it was enjoyable, just being with you.

And now that's what my life seems to be: an effort. Work to find things to fill my time. I have plenty I CAN do, but little that inspires me or that is enjoyable.

I need to find contentment again. I need to find fulfillment in something. I need to find happiness in a world without my best friend.

And I need you here to help me, to talk me through the toughest time of my life. I need my best friend to help me through this, to help me as you did for all our years together. I need you here to help me cope with your loss.

February 25, 2018

Dismembering Your Life

I'm moving on.

I've taken pictures of your office, as you had it when you were here. It's my attempt to maintain your memory. The office was you: your art, your collections, your special retreat filled with all your favorite things, gadgets, technology.

Your blue chair – the ugly Early American monstrosity – is still there where it was relocated after many an argument when you rescued it from your mother's basement. NO. It CANNOT stay in our living room! I disagreed with having it in the house, let alone our modern Ikea-furnished living room. Finally, you capitulated (after how many arguments?) and removed it to your office.

And now, years after our disagreements, nearly seven months after your death, I cannot bear to see it removed from the house.

I gave Cindy your Chromebook. I gave the kids and George your coats and shoes. I'll find somewhere to donate your awards. I'm sure someone can re-use the frames (and you were planning to get rid of them anyway).

I think I'll move the long table you built into my own office. I'll take back the iMac that we both agreed should be yours once you retired from Delta and were home working on website business all day. It was only fair that you have the nice computer since I would be working at the office 40 hours a week and you'd be working at home.

After removing the table and the computer, I'll probably put a bed in there and your office will no longer officially be your office. It'll be the guest room.

I'm being practical. You aren't coming back. If you're here with me now (and I feel you here, often, don't I?)…if you're here, you're saying, "Do what you want, honey. Be practical, Ger. I'm not coming back and there's no point in keeping it a shrine to me."

And I know this. I know you won't be back. I know you're gone and I need to process your death, your absence, my new existence as a widow. I know this.

But I feel like with every action I dismember what you built, what you created, a part of you. I'm dismembering our life together, the things you made special here in our home.

I'm leaving you behind day by day.

And I want to scream, NO! NO NO NO NO NO! He can't be gone. It's not fair. It's not right. The man I loved must be just around the corner, just down the hall, in his favorite space. He's in there creating some new website, designing a new sign or newsletter or logo. He's editing pictures he took with the camera he loved so much. He's listening to Paul Simon songs or practicing playing "Superman" on his guitar. He's surfing the web, or he's playing Pipe Dream on the old PC he bought to play his beloved 70s video games. He's racking up his Tetris score and about to call me in to see it.

Isn't he?

And I'll yell out, "What are you doing?" And he'll yell back, "Waiting for you."

And we'll go to lunch at our favorite diner, or, better yet, we'll take a Sunday nap together and I'll get to hold him again.

But none of that is true, is it?

Instead I'm dismantling your office. Removing one more thing you created. Dismembering what you built.

I'm moving on.

February 25, 2018

Hope

Hope.

I didn't want to get out of bed this morning. It happens.

I lay there contemplating why. Why today? Why is it so difficult to get up this morning?

I realized that today I feel no hope. No hope of ever enjoying my life again. No hope for a future that is meaningful. No hope of ever feeling right or complete without Rick in my life. No hope of feeling happiness. No hope of true joy or fulfillment, all because my life partner is gone.

I feel dead inside.

My counselor says hope is the reason for living, that studies have proven people who have hope live through horrific events. Hope keeps us alive.

And that sums up how I felt, as I strove to rise, as I fought my way out from underneath my covers – I felt hopeless and unable to keep on living.

I pushed myself and I arose. I set off to work. I talked myself through the process. I told myself that I've felt this way before, and the feeling changes, and I do go on. I have to. I will.

And, hours later, I think I realized why today, why this morning, I may have felt this sense of loss so greatly.

Every day, I watch last year unfold before my eyes through Facebook and Timehop memories. We were in Florida, watching sunsets. We were at outdoor restaurants, eating pizza and drinking wine. We were basking in the light of remission. We were hopeful.

Rick was going to beat the cancer. He had gone through the trials and made it. He wasn't cured, but the chemo and radiation had worked – it had destroyed the tumors and all he had left to endure was the brain radiation that would hopefully circumvent any chance of the tumors spreading to his brain.

WE HAD HOPE.

We thought we had more time. We talked about taking a three-week trip across the upper northwest in the fall. Short-term, we decided to return to Florida at the beginning of April, when his brain radiation would be complete – and he'd be done with it all, the tests, the treatments, the hospitalizations. It would all be over and we could reclaim our lives.

We were so wrong. And now he's dead, and I'm alone. What do I possibly have to hope for?

March 2, 2018

Miles – a poem I wrote to Rick in May 1996

I wrote this poem when Rick and I had been dating for a little more than two months. He lived in Minnesota and I lived in Michigan, and he was often in various parts of the country for his job. I sent it to him as part of an email message. He printed it and saved it, and I found it among his things.

At that early stage of our relationship, we were both already deeply in love, and knew we wanted to spend the rest of our lives together.

Miles

Distance cannot stop my love
From seeking your heart's strings.
Our souls communicate past miles,
And mine to yours still sings.

The great expanse of country
Can't keep our love apart.
For still I feel you near me;
I sense you in my heart.

My mind's eye beckons you at will.
I see you in my dreams at night.
I hold you in my fantasies
And feel your kiss at morning's light.

You may be far away in fact,
And for your touch my body yearns,
But in my soul, I hold you close,
And love you with a force that burns.

March 3, 2018

As I read the poem today, I realize the sentiment still holds true now that he's gone from me forever. He may be far away in fact, but I still sense him in my heart. I decided to update the poem and the new version is on the next page.

Distance Cannot Stop My Love
(formerly "Miles" – revised)

Distance cannot stop my love
From seeking your heart's strings.
Our souls communicate past death,
And mine to yours still sings.

The great expanse of heavens
Can't keep our love apart.
For still I feel you near me;
I sense you in my heart.

My mind's eye beckons you at will
I see you in my dreams at night.
I hold you in my fantasies
And feel your kiss at morning's light.

You may be far away in fact,
And for your touch my body yearns,
But in my soul, I hold you close,
And love you with a force that burns.

March 4, 2018

Our First Date Anniversary

Dear Rick,

I made it through another significant day. Our first date was March 9, 1996. We celebrated the occasion every year, and yesterday was a tough one.

I had to pause a few times during the work day to cry. I just miss you so terribly that I can't stand it. I think back on that date and know that we both were aware of how strong the attraction was. I remember thinking that just maybe you were "the one."

We both knew the first date rules. You meet somewhere public for a cup of coffee. That way, if you can't stand each other, you have an easy and quick date, then escape out the door. We both hated coffee and agreed to meet for diet Cokes. We met at the Ram's Horn in the vestibule. You said, "Oh, it's you! Wow, you're beautiful." What a first line! LOL. I was hooked.

As we were about to enter the restaurant, you stopped and asked, no, would I rather go somewhere else? And I agreed, and we went to the Wheat and Rye instead.

So we met and got a booth in the corner. You were so interesting and funny and intelligent. Always the consummate interviewer, you plied me with questions about me and my life and – as the night went on – you were more and more excited about how much we had in common and how much our interests gelled.

Finally, later in the evening, you asked what my favorite food was. I told you Mexican food, and you laughed and asked, "Will you marry me?"

It was a joke, and I laughed, too, but we both knew by then that we were hooked. I took a break to go to the ladies' room and I remember smiling and rehashing that comment, that joke you made: Will you marry me? And I thought to myself, Yes, maybe I will.

We talked and talked for hours, without pause. We talked about writing, and our work, and our kids, and our pasts. The night flew by and you kissed me goodbye in the parking lot. The date was over, but I knew neither of us wanted it to be, so I invited you back to my apartment. And we stayed up all night.

And 22 years later, I'm still surprised at how lucky I was to have met you, to have loved you, to have become one with you forever. You're part of me now and always will be.

I love you, honey. Happy first date anniversary.

XXOO

March 10, 2018

I'll Be Seeing You

I made it through day one of my driving trip from Michigan to Florida. I had three small meltdowns triggered by songs on the radio, plus some memories that surfaced as I passed through locations we visited on past trips.

Three days ago was the seven month anniversary of Rick's death. In the months after he died, I never imagined that I'd go back to Florida this year. I feared how painful it would be to experience a vacation and sunsets without him. But once I started seeing all the memories of last year pop up on Facebook and Timehop, I realized I can't and won't avoid those memories. The final impetus was when Rick's daughter told me she imagines that his spirit is on the beach in Florida waiting to see me.

And that's when I realized, Rick would want me to go. Rick would tell me to get out and live my life – as he lived his! He survived months of chemo and radiation and still got in that car last year despite low blood counts and the exhaustion from enduring so much. I wouldn't have had the strength to do what he did every single day before his body finally gave out. He rose from that bed and tried! He tried to walk, to build his strength, and to live in the moment, every moment.

I feel really positive about my decision to go and enjoy the place we loved and the memories we shared. But, I think since I decided to go, I've just been on autopilot – getting things ready and making my itinerary, packing, arranging the house sitters. As I started the car in my driveway today, and it became real, I thought – What the hell am I doing? This is going to hurt! I can't do it!

It probably will be painful, but every day hurts living in the home we shared. Every time I go to the places we dined and shopped, it hurts all over again. But I know he's going with me, and I know he'll be there on the beach beside me, so I drove down the street and got on the highway.

When I checked into my hotel tonight, for no reason, the old song from the 1940s, "I'll Be Seeing You," popped into my head. I started singing it to myself and caused meltdown #4. I hadn't thought of this old standard in years, and it certainly fits how I feel about this first trip to our favorite vacation spot without Rick by my side.

I'll find you in the morning sun, and when the night is new. I'll be looking at the moon, but I'll be seeing you

March 16, 2018

Day 2: Jack in the Box

Day two of my solo journey started out okay. I awoke to great weather in Bowling Green, Kentucky – warm and sunny. It was strange packing the car by myself. I always traveled with Rick and he usually packed while I finished dressing. I'll admit, Rick spent most of our marriage finding things to do while waiting for me.

Our usual conversation – Me: What are you doing? Rick: Waiting for you.

An hour's drive down the highway from the hotel was the Jack in the Box where we always stopped. As Michiganders, we were both introduced to the JIB taco when we were teens, then, quite suddenly, the corporation left the state – in fact, just about all of the states east of the Mississippi. When Rick and I met years later, we discovered that we both had a love of Jack in the Box tacos (it's definitely an acquired taste. lol). When Rick traveled for work, he'd bring some home on his flight from California. By the time he arrived in Michigan, the bag was usually filled with soggy tacos, but beggars can't be choosers.

So the JIB stop was a huge part of our trip. We'd eat some in the restaurant, then take dozens to go in our cooler to eat in the ensuing days of travel.

This was a tough one, going into the restaurant alone. I decided I didn't want to eat there, and ordered some to go. I went out to the car, rolled down the window and took a bite. There was no joy. Oh, it tasted good, but the fun of being there with him, enjoying something that brought us both memories of our youth, watching Rick play air guitar – that's what made that part of our trip special.

How many times will this happen on my solo trip? Too many, I assume. I "swallowed" my disappointment and my tears, and set off again.

I guess I was primed for a meltdown, so when "Walking in Memphis" by Marc Cohn, came on the radio, I was a goner. Rick loved that song. Many a road trip when the song came on, he cranked up the radio and started to belt it out. His enjoyment while singing it was infectious, and I'd usually start singing along. It was just another of a million fun memories we shared, one of those memories that brings him back to me so vividly that I can almost feel his presence.

Years ago, when he traveled a lot for work, he sang at karaoke bars across the country and won many awards along the way. He had the perfect husky voice for this song. And when the part came.... "boy are you a Christian? Ma'am I am tonight!" he would sing it with gusto.

So I started singing, fully in the moment, and at that exact part of the song, I lost it.

I was driving and crying and trying to decide if I should pull over, when it happened: the passenger seat belt chime went off. This has happened before, and at odd times, too, with no rhyme nor reason. There was nothing heavy on the seat, and, besides, why didn't it go off when I started the car, or at any other time in the two hours I had been driving? No, it went off when one of his favorite songs came on, after his favorite part, and when I started crying.

So – crazy, hopeful widow that I am, I knew he was with me. I knew his spirit was right there in the car with me, and I told him once again how much I miss him, how much I loved him – still do and always will. I've been talking to him quite a bit this trip. Truthfully, I talk to him at home, too, and I don't know when I'll ever stop. There's one thing I realized today. Maybe it's because I have more time to talk out loud to myself on this long trip, but I noticed that I say a lot of phrases that Rick used to say, using the same inflections he did. *Wow! What a beautiful day, eh?* or *Man, that's a great song!* I even caught myself yelling at a crazy driver: *What the hell are you doing, asshole?*

I guess that's what 20 years of marriage does – and I realized that while driving today, too. In the last decade or more of our marriage, we were so in tune that I wasn't sure where I ended and he started. We finished each others' sentences. We were a united front. There was no "him" and "me" – it was only "us."

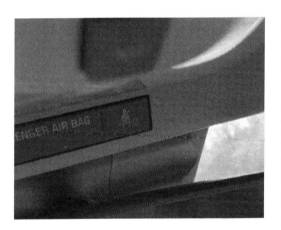

And that's the most difficult part to get used to. As unfair and awful and depressing as it is, I need to navigate this world as just me. Maybe that's why this trip is so important, and so difficult.

I'm at my next stop now. I've checked into a hotel in Alabama, and I only have a few short hours of driving in the morning until I reach our Florida vacation spot. I'm sadder than I was last night. Several times during the day, I vacillated between feeling positive and independent, feeling close to him because I'm reliving the special times we shared, and questioning whether I should have made the trip at all.

It's so awful not having him here, but it's awful at home, too. Most of all, I think I'm where he'd want me to be.

And I think he's here with me, too.

March 17, 2018

The Dream

Dear Rick,

I can't stand it. I can't stand that you're not here with me.

Yes, I'm proud of myself. I drove to Florida. But the pride doesn't count for much when compared to the misery I'm feeling right now.

Not seeing you in the chair next to me at sunset was devastating. You're supposed to be here. And, once again, I'm amazed that you're gone. It happened so fast. Our wonderful life together was here one moment, and torn apart the next.

I know, I shouldn't complain. Many don't have the time we had in the end. The ten months after the diagnosis, when we knew that we needed to make every moment count. But you were in remission, and the way you died so unexpectedly blindsided me. Neither of us were ready for it to happen so suddenly.

And yet, I had a dream the other night about you. You were alive and taking photos in a mall of some sort. But it was me, now, in the present, and I knew what was going to happen and how you were going to die. I knew I was going to get the idea for you to take in the garbage – to practice walking and do a chore, just to make life a little more normal for you. You had been struggling just to rise from your chair, but the day before you had more strength, and that morning you wanted to do something, anything, that was "normal."

And you asked, "What's on the agenda today?" And I suggested, "Why don't you try to take the garbage cans up to the house?" And you were happy, so happy to do that little chore. And you said, "I think I can do that!" And so you went out, and you fell, and died of complications from the fracture. And just like that, you were gone.

And in the dream I knew what was about to come, and I realized I could change the outcome. I could NOT suggest you take out the garbage. I could keep my mouth shut, and change the outcome, and you wouldn't fall, and you wouldn't die.

But in that moment in my dream, I realized that – if I truly loved you – I couldn't try to change anything, because maybe, just maybe, the way you died was a blessing.

Something was wrong in those last months, very wrong. You were having problems with your logic, and the pneumonitis shouldn't have affected your mind that way. You were wasting away, and the doctor said later that the cancer had probably spread somewhere, but we never had the chance for the PET scan to find out.

And I pictured you suffering more, weakening, possibly in pain, dying slowly and horribly, lingering in hospice….and I knew I had to let you die the way you did. I had to sacrifice the time I could have had with you for your sake. I had to let you "go gentle [and suddenly] into that good night." And now I alone rage, rage, against the dying of the light.

March 18, 2018

Do not go gentle into that good night,
Old age should burn and rave at close of day;
Rage, rage against the dying of the light.

From "Do not go gentle into that good night" by Dylan Thomas

Distraction

My life is consumed by grief, by your presence in my memories, by your absence in my day to day existence.

Everything else is an attempt at distraction.

March 19, 2018

August 8th

Dear Rick,

My mind continues to go back to that day last August, the day you called me to come lie with you in bed. I was working from home, as usual, and we had eaten Burger King in the park for lunch. Now it was 4 p.m., and I had just finished my work day in my home office. You had been napping in the bed across the hall. As you so often did in those last days, you called to me and asked me to join you in bed, and I obliged.

As I lay in your arms, you said, sadly, "I think we should close the business."

I objected. I didn't want you to work if you didn't want to, but I knew that growing our business had been so important to you. You gave your all to the customers we had and to finding new clients, as well. You even scheduled new client meetings around your early chemo appointments. I think I was panicked. I thought this meant you felt defeated, that there was no hope, so I protested the idea.

You said quietly, softly, "Honey, I don't know how long I'm going to live."

Those awful awful words play over and over in my memory. You knew. You knew. You knew.

Not one to ever ever give up hope, I suggested that we just cancel the contracts of the customers who required a lot of time and energy, those that needed constant updates. We would keep only the websites that you really enjoyed working on. You loved creating, planning, writing. Why stop it all? And, besides, I said, the idea of transitioning all those clients to new hosts exhausted me. Transferring WordPress sites always involved some type of issue that would need resolving.

Always practical, you said, "No, the clients need to take that up with their new hosts. Companies go out of business all the time. We'll announce that the business is closing at the end of the year, and the clients will need to find new web companies to take over and transfer the sites. You don't have to take care of all that."

Yes, always practical.

A weight lifted off me then. I knew you were right, and I think I wondered if I could go on with the business alone; to work a full-time job and come home to client work would be a lot of stress. But I didn't want to think about a time in the future without you.

I suggested that I put together a list of all our clients, to see which clients were no work at all: the ones who only used us for hosting, the ones who simply paid their yearly fees and required no work from us.

So that evening, at 8:34 p.m., according to the Google Doc version history, I made a list of clients and organized them by those that required work and those that didn't, and I shared the document with you so we could discuss it.

And because I did that, I can put an actual date to the conversation, the words that play over and over and over in my mind: "Honey, I don't know how long I'm going to live."

That evening was August 8, 2017. That evening was two days before you fell and broke your hip, five days before you died.

And I wonder now, why did I focus on the business part of the conversation? Why didn't I ask how you felt about what you'd just said?

"Honey, I don't know how long I'm going to live."

Oh I'm pretty sure I had some type of response to that remark. I think I said something like, "well, none of us knows," or some other inane, pat, easy answer, because I thought that was how you wanted it. You didn't seem to want to talk about the reality of your death. You talked about being so lucky that the cancer was found early, that maybe that bode well and that it wouldn't return. That maybe you'd be in the 10 percent who survived.

I wonder so many things now. I have lots of time to wonder. Was all that hopeful talk for you or for me?

I remembered another thing recently. I remembered something you said to me in our first months of dating. I was happy about something and you asked, "Do you ever get sad? Because I don't think I could stand to see sadness in your eyes."

Many times in the past twenty-one years, you saw sadness in my eyes. We survived loss and grief and life together. And if you're here with me now, you're seeing lots of sadness, unspeakable sadness.

I'm rehashing and questioning so much: "Honey, I don't know how long I'm going to live."

Why didn't I ask how you felt about that? Why you felt that way that particular day? If you really wanted to do something else with your time? If you wanted to talk, have a real talk, about the possibility that your death was imminent?

Did you know? Did you know you only had a few days?

But I didn't ask.

March 19, 2018

wid·ow
/ˈwidō/
noun
1. a woman who has lost her spouse by death and has not remarried.
2. PRINTING
   a last word or short last line of a paragraph falling at the top of a page or column and considered undesirable.

verb
1. make into a widow or widower.
   "she had to care for her widowed mother"

Widow

Yesterday was day two of my stay in Florida – my first trip driving by myself from Michigan, my first vacation without Rick.

I was sitting on the beach alone, watching the sunset and missing him, trying to feel him, thinking only of him.

My friend Traci called from Michigan to check on me. She knew this was going to be difficult for me. I told her about my three-day driving trip. I expressed how surprised I was that I felt no trepidation about driving by myself, but that I had quite a few small meltdowns when the memories hit, when I felt anew that he was truly gone and I'll be making these solo journeys the rest of my life.

I told her about sensing him with me in the car in Tennessee, after Walking in Memphis came on the radio, that when I started to cry, the passenger seat belt sensor came on. It was my confirmation that he was there. My friend believed me. She agreed that he was there with me.

Traci is one of my biggest fans and supporters. I've known her my entire life, since I was four, and she's always had my back. In fact, when I was so fearful of my first date with the man I met on the internet twenty-two years ago, she was the one who talked me through the day and encouraged me to meet him. I did and I met my soulmate. Rick and I were married a year later.

At the end of our discussion, she posed a question for me to consider. She said it seemed in blog posts and Facebook posts, and in general, I refer to myself as a widow quite a bit. She said you were a whole person; you were you, before you were Rick's wife. She asked if I was too focused on being his widow.

I've been contemplating that question since we talked, and I thought about how the word "widow" itself has evolved in meaning for me.

When Rick first died, I had to make the usual numerous phone calls regarding life insurance, credit cards, pensions, and more. They were difficult to make, and my brain was truly fogged. But I do remember one instance where the person I called asked who I was, how I was related to "the deceased." I stumbled on the answer. I started to say I was his wife and choked on a sob, corrected myself, and said I was his widow.

I hated saying that. I hated it with a passion. I wanted to scream into the phone, "I am his WIFE! I always will be! I don't care if he's not here physically. I'm his wife. I wear his ring. I am connected to him."

Calling myself his "widow" forced me to acknowledge that he's dead.

But now, seven months later, I think I've started to embrace the term. I am the widow of a wonderful man named Rick Palmer. He existed and being his widow tells the world that he did. I am not a single woman; I am a widow who loved and became one with my husband. I tell this to the world by using that nomenclature.

And more significantly to me, as I told my friend, Rick was half of my life. Yes, I was a whole person when I met him, but I am not a whole person yet. I'm working toward that, but I'm too early in my solo journey – physically, mentally, and emotionally. Although I am working hard to fill my time with my own needs, to discover my own wants again, to live my life alone and create a future for myself, in all honesty, the majority of my day is consumed with thoughts of Rick, with memories of his love and life, and with a yearning to be with him again.

Rick was a huge man literally and figuratively. He was 6 foot 5 inches tall and weighed between 300 and 350 pounds at different times throughout our marriage. He was a tall mass of muscle. He also had a larger than life personality: he loved life with a passion, he had a soul that sought adventure, and he created brilliant writing and designs. He was fun, exuberant, loud, and quirky.

This "larger than life" man left a very large hole in me and in my existence, and it will take a lot of effort and time to fill it.

So, for now, I refer to myself as a widow. I feel like a widow. I am a widow. It's strange how I've come to embrace a term I so dreaded immediately after his death, but now it fits.

Hopefully, with the help of my grief counselor, with work on my part, and with the passage of time, some day in the future, I'll be myself again and I'll feel whole. But for now, seven months after his death, I am foremost a woman whose husband died.

I am a widow.

March 20, 2018

I'm Glad I Made the Trip

Dear Rick,

I'm glad I made the trip.

Having made the journey is like a big sigh of relief – now. It wasn't that way at first. It was a challenge, a thing I knew I had to do to reach closure, to continue with my new life.

A new life I didn't ask for or want.

The first evening, when I arrived and rushed to gather my beach chair and things to take to the sunset, I felt your loss more than I had in months. I was knocked to my knees with grief. I collapsed on my bed in the fetal position. I was devastated by the sheer and utter pain that overwhelmed me.

I could not do it. I could not go to our most special place on earth without you.

Those sunsets we viewed together last year when you were in remission were the epitome of our love and life and marriage and the world we built and shared together. But they were bittersweet. Although we both tried valiantly to hope for the best, in my heart, I knew you would be gone this year, and I knew it would be our last trip together.

I experienced what I now know was anticipatory grief, and when the fear and the sadness threatened to overtake the joy, I had to remind myself over and over that I would have plenty of time to grieve later. Enjoy the moment. Enjoy the time spent holding your hand on the sandy beach. Enjoy our banter. Enjoy your hugs. Enjoy you.

And I did.

And I was right: you aren't here this year. And I was right: I have plenty of time to grieve now.

And when I readied myself for the big moment – my first sunset on the gulf without you, the overwhelming fear shocked me to the core. No, I cannot go on without you…no, I cannot go revisit our special special place without you…no, I can't do it! And I lay on the bed quaking. I thought I must call someone, my son, my niece, my best friend – someone must save me. I can't do this alone. I can't breathe.

But in my heart, I knew no one could save me. I knew I had to go on without you. I have no choice. And the sun will continue to set on the gulf without you. And the sun will rise again tomorrow without you. And I will continue my life without you.

And going to that first sunset hurt like hell. But I did it. And I survived, and I will go on with my life – without you.

March 23, 2018

Who Am I?

Who am I?

It's been nine days since I left Michigan to go on my first solo drive to Florida, and I'm now on the way back home.

As the trip progressed, I started to feel more like myself, but also like a new person. There are things about traveling alone that I liked intermingled with times I was lonely and missed Rick terribly.

This morning, I had to rearrange my plans because I mistakenly only reserved six nights at the motel where I'm staying. I had planned to stay seven, so I suddenly was confronted with checking out this morning and deciding what to do and where to go next. But this sudden change of plans made me realize that I felt a sense of empowerment I had not felt since Rick's death.

I can go anywhere and do anything I like.

So I pondered ideas.

How about I go to the place we used to go, about 1 ½ hours north of Treasure Island, and revisit that place? Get another bit of closure?

But I don't want to miss this final sunny, warm day, so how about if I go and lie by the pool and read when I get there? That way I'll be sure to have one more day of sun and relaxation before heading back to frigid Michigan.

My friends had offered to let me stay at their place when I checked out Sunday. When I told them I was checking out on Saturday, they extended the offer to the extra day. But I didn't want to stay with anyone. I like staying by myself. I like the independence. I like planning my day totally around my desires for the day. I don't want to be polite, or work around others' schedules, likes, and dislikes.

If I have to live my life alone, I need to do it my way.

If I have to live without my love, let me enjoy it the best I can.

I packed, stopped by to say goodbye to my friends, and decided to stop for a sandwich and work out my next steps. Where would I stop next? What hotel would I stay at?

I sat and enjoyed my lunch while I searched online. The motel where Rick and I used to stay was full. In all honesty, it had some rough elements staying there – there were some drunken episodes a couple of nights when we stayed there last time, so maybe it was for the best. I stayed at a nicer place just down the road. It cost $30 more, but I'm justifying paying more for hotels because I'm traveling so much more economically as a lone traveler – and safety is my priority.

I drove to the hotel, unpacked, decided I'd like a swim, then decided I'd like to sit in the sun and read Sue Grafton's last novel. It became a bit chilly as the sun was about to set, and I felt like having a nice hot shower and relaxing a bit. I became hungry, and went to Hardee's – one of Rick's favorite vacation fast food joints – first time without him, and more closure.

I ate there, working on a crossword puzzle. (I also noticed that there were two other separate single adults eating alone – something I'm noticing more, now that I'm paying attention.) I finished, gassed up the car in preparation for leaving early tomorrow, and was driving down the street, headed back to the hotel, when I suddenly asked out loud with some surprise, "Rick, who am I?"

Who is this woman contentedly traveling alone in a state 1200 miles from home? Who is this woman who drove there herself, spent a week vacationing alone, visiting beaches, and restaurants on her own? This woman who met a new friend from Facebook for drinks, met friends for various evenings out – cards, trivia, and dancing – and then returned to her own motel room to relax and write?

Who is this confident, SINGLE woman?

Who am I? What will I do next?

The sky's the limit.

Yes, I still miss Rick terribly. Yes, many times throughout the day, I am stunned anew that he isn't with me. I feel his loss, my loss. On this trip, I missed my travel companion and I often felt lonely.

But I'm also beginning, just a little, to enjoy the adventure. As the grief still flows around me, I have more times of hope – hope that maybe I'll be alright, that maybe I will feel joy again someday. I'll just keep moving forward – alone – because I have no other choice.

Somewhere along the route, maybe I'll discover me.

March 24, 2018

Trevor Noah on Grief...

On my drive from Michigan to Florida, I listened to the end of Trevor Noah's beautiful memoir, *Born a Crime: Stores From a South African Childhood*. When he described the pain he felt upon hearing that his mother had been shot in the head, his words resonated with me immediately.

I had to pause the book so I could take in how brilliantly he described my very own pain upon Rick's death.

And then I cried tears as I had never cried before. I collapsed in heaving sobs and moans. I cried as if every other thing I'd cried for in my life had been a waste of crying. I cried so hard that if my present crying self could go back in time and see my other crying selves, it would slap them and say, "That shit's not worth crying for.'

My cry was not a cry of sadness. It was not catharsis. It wasn't me feeling sorry for myself. It was an expression of raw pain that came from an inability of my body to express that pain in any other way, shape, or form.

I have often felt this pain over the past few months, and I had had these very thoughts: how often in my life did I cry over what I now perceive to be nothing in comparison? How many useless boys did I cry over as a teen? How many times did I cry in self-pity over issues that seem minimal now?

Nothing compares to the pain I felt upon losing my soulmate, my lover, my best friend, my world, my Rick.

March 27, 2018

Excerpt from *Born a Crime: Stores From a South African Childhood,* by Trevor Noah. Publisher: Trevor Noah (January 1, 2017)

If I could have you back for one day – A Poem

If I could have you back for one day…

I'd hold you and never let go.
I'd bask in your love
I'd dance in your arms
And tell you that I love you so.

I'll ask you to tell me stories
Just to hear your deep voice again
It's been so awfully quiet
Without you here…

And then…

I'll lie in bed cuddling you close
My head on your broad, muscled chest,
Listening to your rhythmic heartbeat
Relishing your warmth as we rest.

I'll whisper how much I love you,
As I trace every line on your face
And sense how perfect the world is
Now that you're back in your place.

I'll nuzzle your neck and kiss you
And entwine my legs with yours
I'll soak you in
I'll feel your love

And be at peace once more.

You'll tell me that you'll never leave me
Even though we'll both know that's not true.
Just give me one day to pretend
That I'll spend my whole life with you.

To Richard Kevin Palmer, 1953-2017, March 27, 2018

Saturday Afternoons – A Poem

You used to say you loved to hear the rain outside our window
On Saturday afternoons spent in bed

A nap became a perfect world inhabited by two

Legs entwined, my head on your massive muscular chest,
Warmed by your love
We talked of everything and nothing

"Let's pretend we're living in our truck. We're traveling the country.
We're snuggled under blankets, napping in the truck bed," you'd say.
"We're vagabonds."

And you'd pull the ratty old blanket – the one you wouldn't let me discard – up under our chins in our imaginary cocoon

"Listen to the train. I've always loved hearing trains in the distance," you'd say.

And I'd snuggle closer in your arms
And I'd cherish your romantic soul.

Kisses and caresses
Strokes and imaginings

Oneness
Wholeness
Contentedness

Illness
Death
Loneliness

Today is a rainy Saturday
And I am transported back to

Our perfect world

Alone in our bed
Under the ratty old blanket

Your words echo in my head
memories cause such incredible pain and longing that I'm not able to breathe

But after the sobs subside, what remains is pleasure
at what we had,
At what some will never find.

Alone in our bed
I still talk to you, still feel you, still sense you

And you are here with me again
And the real world means nothing

March 31, 2018

Thirst – A Poem

God, I want to touch you again

The photos and videos aren't enough
The memories aren't tangible
The words that echo in my head don't slake the incredible thirst, the longing, the need, the desire

To touch you
To hold you

To lay the length of my body against yours
To run my hands down your massive chest, through the thick mat of hair
To move my hand slowly down down down
To know all of you,

every inch, every warm, pulsing, alive portion of your beautiful hard, strong body

That is no more
That will never be again

God, I want you to touch me again

I want to lie in the cocoon of your love
And feel you caress me

To start at the top of my head and smooth my hair back from my face
And look deep into my eyes

And we are one
And we will always be

Then stroke down down down
And know all of me

And when you died, my life ended

And heaven does not exist for me
And hell is real

Because I cannot touch you again.

March 31, 2018

Scraps

I can't hang onto you, I know that.
But I'm trying.

I'm trying so hard to move on, when everything inside me screams -
hang on, hang on, hang on to every scrap, every piece of him

As your life is being dismantled.

I want to keep every aspect of your life untouched, in place.

I know you don't need your clothes, your shoes, your files
You don't need anything now.

But I do.
I don't want to lose you.
So I keep the scraps, the mementos, the photos, the things you kept because you liked them.
Your stuff.

But it doesn't help.

Gone eight months now. It seems like eight years. I miss you more each day.

Each day, you slip farther away. When I return to the empty house, I don't expect you to be home anymore, waiting, with dinner on the grill.

When I wake up in the morning, I'm used to you not being here, in your office - the early riser waiting for me, the sleepy head.

When I enter our empty bed, I no longer try to pretend that you are behind me, waiting for me - the night person - waiting to envelope me in your strong arms and pull me to you.

I did a little pretense yesterday.

I was sitting in the park, on a sunny Sunday afternoon, reading my book - just the way you liked to do.

A man rode towards me on his bicycle - a large man wearing a helmet.

For one fraction of a second, I hoped it was you - and then I remembered that you are gone.

And I said to myself, just for a minute, pretend it's him. Just for a minute, pretend you are meeting him as you so often did when he was out riding on the weekend.

Just for one shining moment, picture him coming towards you, smiling, as happy to see you as you are to see him.

Just pretend he's alive and life is still perfect.

So I did.

For one short minute, perhaps only 30 seconds, I allowed myself to fantasize, to dream that my lover was back, coming towards me, smiling.

And then the man turned on his bicycle and rode away.

And my life was empty again.

April 9, 2018

To Rick: I Wanted to Grow Old With You – A Poem

I wanted to grow old with you, but fate had other plans.
I vowed to love you until death as we stood holding hands.
We pledged to be together until our lives were through.
I thought we'd spend the golden years ahead, just me and you.

I know you'd be here if you could, you tried so hard to live.
You struggled to rise every day, gave all you had to give.
If love alone could save you, you'd still be here with me.
If love alone could bring you back, how lovely life would be.

But no one lives forever, so I go on alone.
I'm finding my "new normal," attempting to move on.
The silence now is deafening, the empty bed brings tears
I dream of you most every night; I hope I will for years.

I look for signs that you're around, perhaps I've gone insane
But I miss you so desperately, I'll grasp at anything.
Our memories are all I have; I guess they'll have to do.
I'm thankful for the years we had; so grateful I found you.

I know that I am fortunate, that some will never know
A love like ours, the joy we shared, before you had to go.
I miss your touch, your gentleness, your laughter, and your care
And now the pain at what I've lost is more than I can bear.

Our vows still echo in my head from on our special day
Our wedding song exactly voiced the words we longed to say…

You sang, "Grow old along with me,"
You said the best was yet to be.
We vowed til death that we'd be true
I wanted to grow old with you.

April 10, 2018

Time, Grief, and an Apple Watch

I just unpaired my husband's Apple Watch from his iPhone. He loved that watch, so it hurt to do it. It's just one more task to take care of after his death, one more step forward as I work through my grief.

It's interesting how today's state-of-the-art technology affects my grieving process. I picture my grandmother and wonder what her emotional triggers would have been after the death of her mate. She probably got teary-eyed when she looked at old photo albums, or the pipes he used to smoke, when she looked down at her wedding ring, or just maybe, when she looked at his old stopwatch and watch fob.

Those types of memorabilia affect me, too, but with a more modern spin: digital photos, videos, websites he designed, his iPhone containing all his games, ebooks, audiobooks, and text messages… and his Apple Watch.

Rick was a technophile. He had the first iPod, the first iPad, the first Android phone, and then he switched to the iPhone, and once he made the switch, he decided to try the Apple Watch. I thought it was an interesting gadget, but wasn't as impressed as he was. Nevertheless, he was excited to buy this new toy, and one thing I loved about Rick was his enthusiasm for just about everything in life, including new technology.

At the time, neither of us realized that in a few short months, he would be diagnosed with small cell lung cancer, and that this would be his last tech purchase. So, Rick got his Apple Watch and he loved it! He enjoyed getting the zen-like messages reminding him to "breathe." He liked glancing down and being able to read his texts anywhere, anytime, or looking to see who was calling when he didn't want to pull out his phone in company.

He was always fiddling with it, showing me apps he was trying, and enjoying each new discovery about what his new toy could do. His enthusiasm was infectious, and I was happy that he was so tickled with the watch during the months he suffered through the tests, chemo, transfusions, and radiation, and then the treatments' side effects.

As Rick grew weaker over the last three months of his life, he was hospitalized quite a few times. On one of those occasions, as he lay in the emergency room bed, he asked if I'd like to wear his watch while he was in the hospital.

I didn't know how to react. Did he have a premonition that he wouldn't make it? Why would he offer his beloved watch to me now? The idea of separating him from the watch that was always on his wrist, and that was now so much a part of him, depressed me. I was suffering from what I now know was anticipatory grief, and I didn't want to be reminded about a time in the future where I'd be sorting his things, putting away his gadgets. But I saw that he wanted me to wear it, and I knew that it would make him happy if I did.

I tentatively agreed to pair the watch with my iPhone until he was released. I said it would give me an opportunity to test it out for myself, to see if I wanted to get one. I ended up having the watch for about three days, and then I quite happily returned it to him.

And now he's gone. And I have his watch forever.
But, oddly, when I first picked up the watch about two weeks after his death, it wouldn't work. It just wouldn't turn on, or charge at all. I tried it on a different charger, I tried resetting it. Nothing.

And then a very old memory came back to me. I thought back to the old song we used to sing in grade school, "My Grandfather's Clock." I remember as a young girl becoming sad as we sang it in music class. I guess I've always been an old soul. I'm the family genealogist. History and death and cemeteries have always been of interest, and this quiet dirge made me think about the transience of life and the imminence of death even as a young girl.

My grandfather's clock was too large for the shelf,
So it stood ninety years on the floor;
It was taller by half than the old man himself,
Though it weighed not a pennyweight more.

It was bought on the morn of the day that he was born,
And was always his treasure and pride;
But it stopped short — never to go again —
When the old man died...

It rang an alarm in the still of the night,
An alarm that for years had been dumb
And we knew that his spirit was pluming for flight
That his hour of departure had come

Still the clock kept the time
With a soft and muffled chime
As we silently stood by his side
But it stopped, short, never to go again
When the old man died.

As the song played in my head, I had an odd thought – just as the grandfather clock had died in this song from more than a century ago, this

Apple Watch stopped, never to go again, when my husband died. I'm not sure when it stopped. It was on his desk at home the weekend he died in the hospital. Did it stop when he took his last breath? As "his spirit was pluming for flight"? It's difficult to imagine relating this technological marvel to the old grandfather's clock in the ancient song, but in matters of death and the spirit, my mind tends to ponder just about everything. Of course, this being the 21st century, and me being a practical consumer, I will return the watch to the repair center to see if it can be fixed. I want to wear it. I want this reminder of my tech-savvy husband. I know he'd be happy that I decided to use it.

So today, in preparation for sending it out for repair, I followed the directions and unpaired the watch from his iPhone (yes, eight months after his death, I still haven't turned in his phone, but that's another story). When I send the watch, I'll include a little note asking the tech guys if they could please, please, please just swap out the battery, if possible. Please, please, please send back the exact same watch. His watch. The watch that encircled his large, strong wrist, and touched his warm, soft skin while he was still alive. The watch that made him smile when there wasn't a lot to smile about. The watch he fiddled with.

The watch that reminded him to breathe.

I know it's not important, but it means something to me, to keep these small connections to him as long as I can. I know the tech guys will probably toss the note without reading it. If they do read it, they'll think it's silly. But I can hope. I can try.

So many small things become significant now that he's gone. So many tiny things can make or break my spirit.

Yes, I am moving on, eight months after Rick's death. Yes, I am trying to find my new normal. But I still grasp at any means to keep our connection, and it's important to me, very important, that I wear his Apple Watch.

April 11, 2018

The Blue Chair: A Widow's Lament

Since Rick died, every time I look at the ugly blue chair, it elicits a different emotion: regret at the arguments we had about it, sadness that he's gone, and a longing to see him sitting in it again. The blue chair was a significant piece of our history – good and bad.

Rick first mentioned the chair a few years before his mother died. He told me there was an old blue chair down her basement that he really liked and that she said he could have. He said that she had collected quite a bit of stuff and that the basement was a mess, so it would be difficult to get to the chair, but that he wanted to retrieve it some day.

I'd never been allowed in the basement of my mother-in-law's house. Upon her death, I discovered why. She was a bit more than a "collector"; the basement was filled floor to ceiling with antiques, furniture, old clothes, fabrics, and plain old garage sale junk. The light bulbs that no longer worked couldn't be reached from the narrow aisle that allowed access to the laundry room, so the dark, cavernous basement held a variety of mysteries, mounds and mounds of artifacts.

Rick and I were tasked with cleaning out the house. Including repairs, this took us two and a half years. Imagine my surprise as we unearthed furniture from underneath the piles – a pool table, two couches, and several chairs, including the blue chair Rick had expressed a fondness for.

What Rick hadn't mentioned was that the chair was hideous! It was a very large, not-so-attractive bright blue monstrosity from another era. My hipster daughter-in-law thinks it's cool, but didn't take me up on my offer to donate it to her, so how cool is it really?

Yes, it's blue – a very bright blue Colonial-style chair, with wooden embellishments and a pleated skirt. And let's not forget that it comes with a larger-than-life matching ottoman (with the same pleated skirt). When Rick uncovered his prized new possession, my mouth must have been gaping. He took a seat, stretched out, propped up his legs on the ottoman, and grinned. He had at last uncovered the chair, and was thrilled about it.

To say I didn't share in his enthusiasm was an understatement.

This was to go in our basement, right? No, Rick wanted it in the living room. It was the most comfortable chair he had ever sat in. He wanted to enjoy it.

Rick was an extra large man. He was 6'5" of (mostly) solid muscle. His weight ranged from 280 to 350 at various times in our 21 years together. A doctor once told him that he had the largest spine he'd ever seen in a patient. His shoulders could fill a doorway. I guess that for a man so large to find a truly comfortable chair that fit him was an important facet in his life. I get that. I was happy for him – but the living room? The room populated with modern Ikea furnishings? The room done in shades of brown, with the geometric patterned area rug, and modern art pieces? This chair just did not fit the decor!

So we argued, and argued, and argued. I pointed out that we had mutually agreed upon every piece of furniture we'd ever purchased in our marriage, and I did not agree with this one. Rick was adamant that he loved the chair, his comfort was important, and decor be damned.

The chair was moved into our living room. Our "mom and pop" setup was a furniture grouping that consisted of his blue chair, an end table, and my classic brown leather club chair. It looked ridiculous.

And so we continued to argue about the chair – every once in awhile – for years.

Rick in his favorite chair

Rick and I both worked from home – he on our web business, me on the business, plus one day each week for my day job, so we each had our own office. One day, he decided to rearrange his, and he carved out a place in the corner for the chair and ottoman. I'm not sure why, but I wasn't going to question his decision. He moved the chair in, added a reading lamp and a large urn filled with walking sticks (another of his prized possessions found in the basement). He soon could be found many a day sitting in the chair, with his feet up, reading a book, or playing on his Chromebook. He was happy as a clam, and so was I. The war was over.

When Rick was in what I now know were the last few months of his life, he was weak from being weaned off steroids too quickly and it was a great effort for him to rise from any chair. I purchased a cheap, old electric lift chair from CraigsList as an emergency solution. It was ugly – even uglier than the blue chair – but it functioned and at that point, the decor meant nothing to me. I needed to make Rick comfortable and find a way to help him to rise to a standing position so he could work his way to his walker.

The old lift chair was in the living room from July 4th until Rick's death August 13th. In the first week after his death, although still in a fog, I wanted the chair gone, not for any reasons of aesthetics, but because I wanted to remove all traces of Rick's illness: the drugs, the vomit pans, the walker, the shots, the Ensure… everything that reminded me of the cancer, the side effects, and the "sick Rick." I wanted to remember the real Rick, the strong, enthusiastic man I loved, and not have constant reminders of the sorrow and pain I endured watching his life fade away.

So, the lift chair was dispatched to the garage, and guess what this crazy widow wanted in its place? The blue chair. I wanted the blue chair Rick loved so much to be in the living room beside me. It made no sense. But it did. And my niece and nephew humored me and moved the chair and ottoman back into the living room. And it gave me one small bit of peace. One small sense of connection with Rick.

It's eight months later, and about a month ago, I rearranged the living room. Suddenly one night, I couldn't stand sitting across the end table from the empty chair. I never know what wild notion will take hold of me anymore, but at that moment, I just couldn't sit there watching TV with the very noticeable empty chair beside me. I guess at different stages of grief, I'll want different things.

So, at midnight, I dragged the chair back to his office. I rearranged the couch to another wall, and the living room is different than it ever was when he was alive.

I go to Rick's office a few nights a week to use his/our computer, and every once in awhile, when I want to feel close to him, I sit in the blue chair and read a book. I have to admit, it's very comfortable.

I have guests coming for an overnight visit next weekend. Yesterday, I thought perhaps it's time to start changing his office into a guest room. The first step would be to move the blue chair to the basement. I decided that I can't bring myself to get rid of it, but it doesn't have to be in his office. I started to remove the feet so it would be easier to move, and then, suddenly, I just couldn't do it. I experienced that feeling I sometimes get, that painful twinge in the pit of my stomach at the thought of parting with something of his. That sickening dread that sometimes comes over me when I realized he's moving farther back into my past.

And that's when I realized that I can't even move the chair out of his office. I love that chair! I love the memory of Rick so comfortably stretched out in it, sometimes even under a blanket. I can see him relaxed, his massively large feet propped up, content in his special place, reading his book – his very favorite thing to do.

I don't know what will happen in the future, how my mind will evolve as I move on, but, for now, the blue chair stays put in the corner where Rick sat, and I'll figure out another arrangement for my guests.

How can I possibly even consider getting rid of the bright blue skirted Colonial eyesore? It's my favorite chair.

April 16, 2018

The Cure – A Poem

I knew each time I touched you, it could be the last
And I feared with each kiss time was moving too fast

And I held on tightly
And I longed for the cure
But you slipped away slowly
Now the past is a blur

And I longed for the cure that I knew wouldn't come
And I longed for the cure that I knew wouldn't come

We tried to enjoy every second we had
And I held you and loved you and for that I am glad

And we went on vacation
To our place in the sun
But each sunset I feared
That next year you'd be gone

And I longed for the cure that I knew wouldn't come
And I longed for the cure that I knew wouldn't come

And I soaked in your words and I memorized your face
Because I knew that too soon you'd be gone from this place

And time flew by quickly
It wouldn't slow down,
And days became weeks
Until ten months had gone

And I longed for the cure that I knew wouldn't come
And I longed for the cure that I knew wouldn't come

And I hoped and I prayed and I screamed and I railed
But the shots and the pills and the treatments all failed

And I begged God for mercy
And I raged against fate
As your body kept weakening
Until it was too late

And I longed for the cure that I knew wouldn't come
And I longed for the cure that I knew wouldn't come

And despite the remission, you didn't get well
And one morning in August you finally fell

And your hip was fractured
And complications set in
And the doctors all told me
That this was the end

And I longed for the cure that I knew wouldn't come
And I longed for the cure that I knew wouldn't come

So I signed all the papers; there was nothing I could do
And I whispered goodbye and I held on to you

And your life ended
Your suffering is through
But my pain is forever
As I live without you

And I long for the cure that I know won't come
And I long for the cure that I know won't come

April 25, 2018

The Wind Chimes on the Deck- A Poem

The wind blows and your spirit speaks to me

  From the chimes
    under the gazebo
      out on our deck

    When I put your ashes inside (a little teaspoon of you)
I had no idea

How your memory
 would resonate
  with each sound
   throughout my days
    and my nights

    With a gentle nudge upon every breeze,

   Each chord brings
 a soft lull
in my pain

With each tone,
  I hear you call my name

    A whisper
      on the wind

      In the tinkling of the chimes,
  I hear your voice

  across eternity

your love
  speaking to me
    across the barrier
      of time

      A soothing murmur
      in my ear

  I feel you
here

I feel you
  next to me

    I feel you
      loving me

      I feel
      you

April 28, 2018

It's All Just Attempts at Distraction

It's all just attempts at distraction.

All day long every day.

Each hour brings a wrong note – discord and strife because nothing is the way it's supposed to be.

The clock ticks and each moment reminds me of what I lost. All day, my rhythms are off. All day, every day, is wrong, soul-jarringly wrong.

Each second reminds me of you and us and how it should be.

Right now we'd be getting up on a Saturday and welcoming the day together.

Right now, you'd be in your office saying, "C'mon, Ger…I'm hungry. Let's go eat."

Right now, we'd be at the diner, and you'd be across from me, eating an omelet and hash browns (with onions) and reading your NYT on your iPad.

Right now, you'd tell me some factoid you just read, and you'd reach across to take my crossword and fill in some blanks.

Right now, we'd plan our day, our tasks and errands and work and play, and I'd love doing all of it with you, because you are who I planned to spend my time with, my minutes, hours, days, weeks, years, decades with.

You are who I chose to love and laugh and cry and die with.

But you died first.

Right now, you'd be driving and we'd be chatting and we'd be hanging out doing everything and nothing on our Saturday afternoon.

Right now, we'd be enjoying the dinner you grilled on an evening after a long day of work and play.

Right now, we'd be toasting each other out on the deck and we'd agree that we had a good life, the best life, the life we never dreamed we'd have because we found each other and we know how fortunate we are.

And we'd laugh and we'd talk and we'd tell each other our dreams, and we'd kiss and we'd dance. And we'd hold each other close under the stars.

Right now, it's late, and we'd be watching TV and talking about how funny your favorite show was, or how well written that movie was, and you'd say, "I'm going to bed. Don't be up too late." And I'd say, I won't. I love you." And you'd stand and groan and stretch and lean over to kiss me and you'd say, "I love you. Goodnight, honey."

And right now, I'd be joining you in bed, and you'd awaken from your sound sleep and pull me to you, and engulf me in your strong embrace, and hold me.

And love me.

Right now, we'd be lying in each other's arms and talking softly until we fell asleep.

And the cycle would begin again tomorrow, the cycle of a life that will never be again.

You are gone and I have to forget you now.

My new life without you has begun.

But it's all just distraction.

All day long is spent
trying to survive the memories,
trying to create a new life,
trying to fill up the empty days and empty nights since you've been gone.

Right now, I'm trying to fill the next hour without you.

April 28, 2018

An Eternity of Sundays Without Him

Why does it hit so hard sometimes? I move along, I feel myself starting to heal – just a little, and then I'm blindsided with a grief so fresh it feels like he died yesterday.

It's 8 and ½ months today. My heart was shattered on an August Sunday nearly nine months ago. Sometimes it seems like yesterday that he was here. Other times, it feels like years since I've held him.

My grandson Jonas and I were watching Peter Rabbit Friday night and Mr. MacGregor died of a heart attack. Jonas had a million questions, "Why did he fall down? Is he sick? What's wrong?"

Then he said, "The man died… MY papa died. My papa died long, long, long, long, time ago."

Yes, to his little three-year-old mind, last week was a long time ago, so several months must feel like an eternity.

An eternity.

Today I can't stop thinking about Rick, about his love for me, about his boyish charm, about his kindness and intelligence and gentleness, and his unparalleled enthusiasm for life. About things we did together and all the Sundays we shared.

Saturdays, Sundays, the weekends in general, are always the most difficult. We'd be doing this now, we'd be doing that. We'd be together because that's what we did. We spent time together all weekend, every weekend. We liked each other, we loved each other, we had fun together, we worked together. We liked to talk about life, and love, and literature. We chose to spend our lives together and we relished the time spent doing everything and nothing side by side.

And it's not fucking fair that cancer stole that from us.

I'm angry and sad and miserable. I don't want to spend my weekends without him. I found the one person in the world who was my soulmate, the yin to my yang, the person who "got me" – and loved me anyway.

We weren't a perfect couple. We argued, we shouted at each other sometimes. He often irritated me to no end, and throughout the years, I saw numerous eye rolls on his part when I irked him.

But for every single argument or disagreement, there was a renewed sense of awareness that, despite our differences, we could and would move on. We would work it out because the most important thing to both of us was that we had found each other, and we both knew it was worth working through the muck to keep this most priceless gem of a life we had created.

And now it's all gone.

He's gone.

And it hurts like hell to spend this Sunday morning without him. I'm still alive and breathing, and I don't take that for granted, but it takes much more effort to be grateful for that. It's cliche, but a part of me died when Rick died, a part of me that still can't come to terms with the knowledge that he's gone forever.

Each morning, I rise from my bed knowing I will feel the emotional pain of his loss in some fashion during the day, whether dozens and dozens of times – as on weekends – or maybe only a handful of times on the busier days during the week. But I'll feel it, and I can't avoid it.

So I plan activities to keep me distracted, and I strive to find meaning in the life I have left. I visit friends and family, and I write, and I work my 9 to 5 job, and I keep our web business going, and I cook, and I clean. And life goes on.

And then there's a day like today, and I just can't do it. I don't want life to go on. I don't want to move forward. I want to move back to the past where he is.

And I wallow in the pain, and I miss the man I love, and I curl up in a chair and I stare at his picture. I relive the memories we shared, and I give into the self-pity and the sadness.

And in a little while, I'll get up again and start all over on my solo journey.

Because I have no choice.

April 29, 2018

Danger! Grief Triggers Ahead

I just ate a Slim Jim and started to cry. How can eating a dried meat stick bring back painful memories? How do the most innocuous acts trigger grief and pain and sadness?

Is there anything that won't remind me of what I've lost?

A few short weeks after my husband's small cell lung cancer diagnosis, we began chemotherapy. I say "we," although I never had toxins injected into my body. I say "we," but I never experienced the unrelieving series of tests and scans, or having a PICC line inserted into my vein, or nausea, or injections, or blood transfusions, or radiation therapies to my lung and brain.

I say "we" because I was there, watching, enduring, trying to be supportive and strong every step of the way as the man I loved attempted, in vain, to beat an insidious foe.

What does this have to do with a Slim Jim?

When Rick and I spent hours in the infusion center during his months of chemo, I packed snacks for us to eat during the long days. For Rick: anything and everything he desired or his chemo-sensitized stomach could tolerate. For myself: low-carb treats like string cheese, almond packets, and Slim Jims.

Today, eight months after his death and more than a year since his last chemo session, I pulled out a Slim Jim for a quick snack at work. As I wrestled with the stubborn packaging, the memories came back in a rush… sitting across from him in the quiet, dimly lit room, watching as the toxic chemicals dripped into his system, staring at him for hours as he reclined under a blanket, snoring softly.

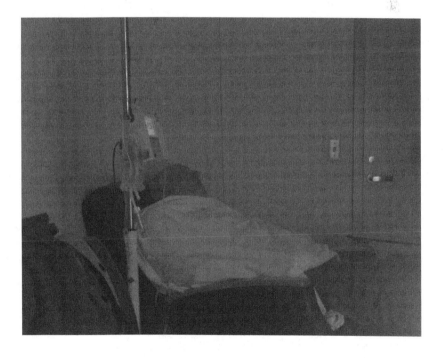

Once again, I experienced the feeling of dread, the constant emotional pain as I wondered and worried and dared to hope, and asked myself how I would live without him if the treatments didn't work.

But then I also recalled his stoicism and his valiant attempts to alleviate my sadness as we visited the basement level of the medical center each day for his 37 lung radiation treatments: him joking and pinching or poking me every time we boarded the elevator and me chiding him and telling him we were on camera and that security would report him for abuse – then reaching to tickle him and both of us laughing and kissing.

In the midst of the most difficult days of his too-short life, he often tried to ease my suffering with laughter, and now that he's gone, the simple act of riding in an elevator brings back those bittersweet memories, too.

An innocuous Slim Jim transported me back to those painful, yet hopeful, times. Days when we both clung to the tiny fragment of hope that Rick would live. Days that were awful, yet better than the empty days I now endure without him.

Days that I thought were the worst of my life, but that I'd live through again if I could, just to see him one more time, hold him once more, hear his voice, once again.

Yes, in an instant, opening a Slim Jim brought all those emotions back in a rush: sadness and tears, hope and longing, pain and fear, laughter and love, leaving me to wonder how I will endure a future in a world filled with so many unexpected triggers.

And knowing I have no choice.

May 1, 2018

Rick horsing around while eating a Slim Jim

The Tulips in Our Yard - A Poem

I see the tulips in our yard
And I remember
When I used to be excited about spring

Spring meant summer was near
And summer meant time outside with you

Days frolicking in the sun
Evenings lounging in the sultry heat out in our yard
Me swatting mosquitoes
You not

Smells and sounds of summer

The scent of chicken on the grill wafting through the air
The grill that lies dormant now

The thump thump of you pounding wood into place
On whatever your latest project is
Fence, deck, enclosure, table, chair, container

The tinkling of your prized fountain
With the water spurting out of the heron's beak

The roar of the lawn mower as you walk back and forth, back and forth
wearing your bright green ear protectors
Hot sun beating down on your arms and back

The tangy salty smell of your skin
When you come to me for a hug, dripping with perspiration
And you laughing as you throw your arms wide and say, Give me a little hug
And me smiling as I accept your taunt
And pull you in close
Sweat and all

And I say, Let's take a swim – you need it

The sound of your antics in the pool
Every day you pretend to slip and slide down the incline into the deep center
Every day, you yell, Whooooooaaaaah!
And dip down beneath the cold water

And every day, I roll my eyes and laugh
Because you are such a nut
You are my nut

And every evening we sit under the gazebo drinking wine
And you say, We should sleep out here
And I say, Okay, let's do it
And you say, We need a lanai, someday we'll have a lanai

But we didn't get a lanai
And we never slept out under the stars in our yard

And we never will
And seeing the tulips in our yard
Reminded me
I used to be excited about spring

Because spring meant summer was near
And summer meant time outside with you.

May 4, 2018

Vestiges of Your Life - A Poem

I cried when I first changed our bed sheets
But any trace of your scent is now gone
I've accepted you aren't coming back
But it's still very hard to move on

Your things are still just where you left them
On the table right next to the bed
The last glass you drank from still sits there
And there's dust on the book that you read

Your box of mints sit on the table
Right next to your favorite chair
And so many times in an evening
I expect to see you sitting there

I know I should clean out your closet
And donate to help the poor
But I still can't help shedding tears
When I fondle the clothing you wore

Each item has a special meaning
Every shirt brings a memory back
Perhaps one day when I'm stronger
I'll remove everything from the rack

Your toothbrush is still in the bathroom
Your shaver's still there on the shelf
I still smell your aftershave often
It hurts but I can't help myself

There are still bits of sand in the car
That I won't vacuum up from the floor
Because every time that I see it
I think of our time at the shore

I'm keeping your cell phone active
Because it's filled with your texts to me
I know it's a foolish expense
But for now, I'll just let it be

I'll admit I still text you sometimes
And I'm not sure exactly why
It gives me some comfort to do it
Even though I won't get a reply

I cuddle up under your blanket
And wear your sweatshirt to bed
And I know I look pretty dumb
With your favorite hat on my head

Yes, call me a crazy widow
But leave me alone to grieve
The love of my life has been taken
And it's still hard for me to believe

May 6, 2018

Sitting Alone at the Coney Island

I'm sitting alone in the booth at the Coney restaurant. I thought I was used to it by now. I thought nearly nine months without you had inured me to eating alone, sleeping alone, existing alone.

But perhaps not.

I miss so much about you and our time together, but I miss chatting with you the most. I want to tell you my observations about the woman sitting in the next booth. I actually almost felt like you were here, so powerful is the urge to speak to you, see you. I almost leaned forward to whisper to you, but your spot in the booth is vacant, like your place in my life now.

None of our conversations were important or contained huge revelations. I just enjoyed hearing your take on life. You always had something interesting to say on any topic.

Sometimes, your stubborn, opinionated comments irritated me. Really really irritated me. We butted heads often. I didn't like when you were negative about life, but your moods never lasted long. (And I may have been a bit pigheaded myself.)

But mostly, I just loved the exchange of ideas and thoughts and relished hanging out with you – and especially at the diner.

So here I am, writing instead of enjoying your company. I can't let myself think beyond the sadness and disappointment of this moment. I can't let myself envision a future of empty booths, or empty chairs, of the empty bed. I can't handle more than this one devastating moment without you, acting pleasant to the waitress, smiling at the other patrons, sobbing inside.

How long will you be ever-present in my mind? On the one hand, it's awful seeing you in my mind's eye all day long and not being able to touch you. It's awful missing you constantly, remembering the things you did and said. It's my living nightmare.

But, when I think of the alternative, that makes me sad, as well. To imagine a time when your memory will have subsided in my mind to an occasional glimmer of the times we spent together, when your memory will become a passing thought in my busy day. To even think of that brings on such a sadness that I'm not sure what's worse – missing you so desperately now or a future where you are no longer a part of my life, a constant presence in my everyday thoughts.

Sufficient unto the day is the evil thereof.

There's definitely wisdom in that aphorism. I doubt the day your memory will have faded will happen very soon, so I'll stick with the misery of today. I'll muddle through the rest of my lunch hour without you, and I'll take one day, even one hour, at a time… until I see you again.

May 10, 2018

Grief Work: A Job I Didn't Apply For

Since my husband died nine months ago, I've been attempting to find my new normal. Like all widows, I'm still getting used to living alone and adjusting to life without my partner, trying to balance taking care of my usual duties while I now take on Rick's, too.

I continue to work full time as a technical writer/editor at the same place I've worked for 22 years. In my spare time, I'm also attempting to maintain the web design company my husband and I started more than 15 years ago, and which was mostly Rick's responsibility. I've reduced the client load to sites that only use our hosting services and require few updates, and I'm not taking on any new business, but the work is still time consuming.

Because I no longer have a man around the house, I'm taking on many of Rick's other "regular duties." After 34 years working for the airline industry, Rick took advantage of an early buyout in 2011 to focus on our business. Design was his joy and his passion, and I'm forever grateful that he spent the last 6 years of his life pursuing what he loved and enjoying his freedom, since he never made it to retirement age. His new schedule meant that he did most of the home maintenance, chores, and errands during the hours I spent at work. He also did all the shopping and cooked nearly every meal, and, wow, I miss coming home to his delicious dinners: grilled chicken, beef stew, Tex-Mex goulash, meatloaf, homemade guacamole and salsa, brats, and cheeseburgers.

Most of our responsibilities were split pretty evenly. I took care of the web business technical duties, budget, and invoicing. Rick ran the rest of the business (the designing, printing, and client needs). I took care of the inside of the house and laundry. He took care of the yard work, gutter cleaning, and car maintenance. I maintained the pool with the chemicals and supplies he toted home from the hardware store. He was also the go-to guy for the household emergencies (like the dead bunny my cat brought into the house and hid last week. I really missed having Rick here to handle that fiasco!).

So, now I'm forced to find time to take on his workload or devise ways to parcel out some of the responsibilities. I'm cooking and running errands that he normally performed. Plus, I made the difficult, decadent decision to use a grocery home delivery service despite the extra cost, since (1) I HATE grocery shopping (Rick loved it!); (2) my time is worth the money; and (3) did I mention I HATE grocery shopping?

My nephew starting doing our yard work when Rick got sick, and he's still taking care of that, so that's a huge relief. He's also helped with several small home repairs. However, I'm beginning to plug away at some of the projects that need finishing around the house: tiling, painting, door molding, finishing the half-done basement, and more.

So, needless to say, each evening and weekend, I have my work cut out for me.

Except I don't seem to be making much progress.

I need to cut and affix about 10 tiles and then do some grouting to finish the kitchen backsplash. The tile, tile cutter, grout, and tools have been sitting on the counter for a month (maybe two). Every weekend, I say this is the one! And instead I spend hours writing blog entries and poems about my grief and how much I miss Rick. I need to paint the walls in the hallway before I finish installing the rest of the door molding. The paint can and rollers are waiting for me on the floor in the hall. The first coat of primer is done, but I never seem to be motivated enough to do the final coat. Instead, evenings often find me curled up in a recliner under Rick's favorite blanket, reminiscing about times we shared and crying quietly to myself.

When I wake up on a typical weekend morning, although there's a list of chores I compiled throughout the week waiting on my desk, I don't get out of bed. Instead, I burrow under the covers, desperately trying to remember the vestiges of a dream about Rick I had the night before, or looking at old photos in the Timehop app on my phone, or reading motivational grief essays on my Kindle. Often, when I get hunger pangs, I realize that it's been several hours since I awoke, and I've been so lost in my thoughts of Rick that I never noticed the time passing.

It's spring and it's time to do the yard clean up. Instead, when I go outside prepared to start on a Sunday afternoon, or in the evening after work, and I end up sitting under the gazebo wearing Rick's hoodie and listening to the wind chime that holds some of his ashes. I talk to him and tell him about my day, just like I used to. The only response is the tinkling of the chimes in the wind.

Then there are the times when I go to the store and sit in the car in the parking lot for a half hour, because a song on the radio reminded me of Rick, and I need to compose myself before I can mingle with others again. On sunny weekend afternoons, instead of accomplishing anything at home, I often drive to our local park – right where Rick and I used to go – just to sit and think about the past and to avoid going back to the empty house. Many weekday mornings, I plan my evening's dinner and whatever I need to do on the latest project, but I scrap the plans and go meet friends for an impromptu dinner instead, then stay out until bedtime, because I don't want to sit home another evening mired in sadness. I'm often late for work or appointments because I find myself lost in thought and discover that a half hour has passed since I remembered something Rick had once said or done, and I'd fallen down the rabbit hole of memories and grief once again.

All of this adds up to lost time and little accomplishment. Plans and goals mean nothing to me anymore, unless it's something that brings him back to me: writing in my journal, composing poems, looking through old photos, digitizing our old videos, or just sitting and thinking, and remembering, and crying.

Those are the types of activities that fill my time now. And you know what? I've come to realize that it's okay.

At my last session with my grief counselor, I expressed my frustration at not accomplishing much. I told her that I waste too much time. I can't seem to get things done. My projects, my goals, my plans, all seem to be in limbo. And she told me something that made sense…she said grieving is work. It takes time and it takes energy, and the process can't be rushed.

She said coping with grief is as much work as having another job.

And I remember now that when we began our sessions shortly after Rick died, she had cautioned me against making any major decisions in this foggy state of early grief, and told me I should also hold off on taking on any new responsibilities or duties.

And now I get it.

I knew "grief work" was a real term, but I hadn't really thought about it as a job. Now that I've experienced the first nine months of the time and effort grief work entails, I can more easily accept that – like it or not – I have added another part-time job to my schedule. The person I shared my life with is gone and my entire life has been turned upside down. Grieving this horrendous loss is time-consuming work that's more vital than all the other plans and projects that will now have to wait. I need to dedicate all the time I can to grieving, to adapting, and to working through the onslaught of memories, new duties, and sense of incredible loss that overwhelms me since I lost my husband.

So I'm stopping with the guilt, and I'm accepting that I can't do it all. I need to focus on my new (and very necessary) job: grieving. This job requires quite a bit of time, and it definitely uses up lots of energy. Grieving is a harrowing job that destroys my schedule, saps my strength, and plays havoc with my emotions.

I would never have taken on this job voluntarily, but it's work that MUST be accomplished. Unfortunately, I can't avoid it, and I have to allow plenty of time to get the job done correctly.

The backsplash will be done someday. The walls will be painted. The molding will be installed. But it may not be any time soon, and I have to accept that. I have another important job that takes precedence in my life, and I need to devote time and energy to processing the thoughts and emotions that consume me. I need to save my energy for the arduous task of grieving.

So, from now on, I'm going to focus on doing the really important things:

I'm going to continue to take time to process my feelings and emotions through writing. I'm going to record my memories of Rick, what we shared, and what I've lost. I'm going to spend evenings sorting through pictures of Rick and letting the memories they trigger wash over me. I'm going to write poetry about my love and loss and dedicate it to him. I'm going to sit outside at night and talk to a wind chime, or look at the moon and remember dancing with Rick outside under the stars. I'm going to sit in my car and daydreaming about the good times, or curl up in my recliner and cry about my loss. I'm going to try to face listening to all the millions of songs that stir up millions of memories and I'm going to sing them softly to myself, or simply sob until the pain is vanquished.

Some evenings, I'm going to schedule time with my loved ones and friends to just hang out and talk. And other times, I'll just sit quietly and feel his presence, and long for the day that I'll see him again.

Yes, I'm no longer going to feel guilt at what I'm not accomplishing, because I'm going to focus on what really needs to be done. These are my important new tasks. This is what my new job entails. And everything else will have to take a backseat, because grieving my husband is the work that matters.

May 12, 2018

The Legacy of the Do-It-Yourselfer

Dear Rick,

Everything in this house elicits a memory. Absolutely everything.

I just heard the clink of the mailbox as the postman left a delivery. We installed the mailbox. We handpicked the perfect one with the perfect finish that matched the outdoor sconces on the garage. We toted it home in the back of your Ford F150.

On a hot summer day, you dug a hole, filled the bottom with cement, put in a 4×4 post, and installed the mailbox on top of it. I aligned the house address numbers and affixed them across the box. You marveled at how straight the alignment was. You stood back, and exclaimed, How did you do that? You didn't use a level or ruler! And I laughed because it's one of the semi-useless talents I've always had that no one in my entire life had ever noticed. But you did, because you were always enthused about the smallest, most insignificant things, and always so supportive and proud of every little thing I accomplished.

And all of those memories flooded back because of the clink of the lid being closed during a simple mail delivery.

I wonder if the memories that surround me in this house are more pungent because we shared in the creation and the work every step of the way. I look at the bookcases we assembled together and remember that we did it twice – once in the house we remodeled in Maryland and again in our house here because we left the first set there because the buyer wanted the "built ins." We loved the look and replicated it here. And I will forever think of you and us as we worked on the project together.

A dozen times every day, I walk through the doorway you widened to make an open floor plan between the living room and kitchen. You and I worked on it together using the sawzall. You taught me again how to build a header – I first witnessed that years ago when you turned a window into a doorwall in Maryland. You amazed me by the things you knew how to do, and the work you accomplished with little fanfare. After you finished the structural parts, we measured and cut the new molding that surrounded it together. I painted it glossy white.

And I remember laughing with you as we did our "thing" – that tradition we started in Maryland. Whatever project we finished, big or small, we walked away a few feet so we could stand back and look at what we had accomplished. You put your arm around me, and I put my arm around you, and we just stood and looked at it and felt pride that we had completed whatever it was. Then gave each other a little hug and a quick kiss and moved on to the next project. It was our little dumb ritual, one we did every time.

Every so often I question what hurts worse. Does it hurt more to stay here, entrenched in the memories? Would it be easier to wipe the slate clean and move to a place that doesn't have so many triggers?

No.

Not yet.

As much as the memories cause pain, they also bring joy. Together, you and I created beautiful living spaces. Together we built a life. As much as it hurts, you're here in everything you touched and toiled to build. You're in the remodeled kitchen, your sweat beading as you ripped out cabinets and ripped up flooring. You're under the widened doorway, muscles rippling as you lifted the header into place while I quickly shoved a 2×4 under it to support it until you could nail it into position.

I picture you vividly everywhere I look in this house. Everything around me brings back memories. And, yes, it hurts. But I wouldn't change a thing, because it reminds me of what we shared, of the world we built together. And those precious memories are all I have left of you.

May 18, 2018

I Want to Keep You Alive

I want to keep you alive. I look around me and I see that there's no way to keep you here, but I'm trying. Life shouts at me, Move on. Move on. Move on...but I don't want to if that means leaving you behind.

I know I can't bring you back. I hate that I couldn't save you, that I wasn't able to change events, or do anything to help stop the cancer's insidious progress. I hated feeling helpless to save the man I loved. I did all I could to comfort and care for you, but it wasn't enough. It would never have been enough, no matter how I rewrite history in my mind. You were dying. The end.

But now, don't I have some control? I can control how much I strive to keep you ever-present in my mind and my life. I can think about you, speak about you, write about you, grieve you daily. I can keep the shirts you wore. I can try to replicate your recipes, or try to finish household projects as you would have wanted them done.

I can gather the things that meant the most to you and cherish them in your memory. I can purchase the furniture we selected together, or choose any new purchases based on what I know you would have liked.

And yet, it still isn't enough. None of those inane attempts to keep you with me will work, because you are gone. Forever.

I'm fighting against the winds of change. I'm fighting an uphill battle to keep your life sacrosanct. I know I'm destined to fail, because time will move on, and you will remain in the past. And oh how that hurts. I want you to stay with me here, but you've moved on to somewhere I can't go, no matter how much I wish it weren't so and attempt to keep you here with me.

You are gone. I want to keep you alive, but I can't.

I have choices to make and things to do. I have new experiences on the horizon. I have options that I can't discuss with you. Well, I try, but I never hear your answer.

That's not entirely true. I do hear you. I knew you so well, I can answer for you. I'm pretty sure I know what your response would be to most given situations.

And do I really want to know what you'd tell me now? Can I face "hearing" you?

You'd tell me that you are dead and that I should live. You'd tell me that my time isn't through and I should embrace every moment I have left on this earth. You'd tell me that life is short – and don't you know that more than most? And you'd say that I should do what I want, and quit worrying. Travel, play, enjoy, live, love.

If you could visit me right now, you'd tell me that you love me and you'd hug me and dry my tears. You'd say there's nothing I can do about the fact that you are gone, and that I should just keep living life to the fullest.

And, oh, how I wish I could.

May 18, 2018

Memorial Day Weekend, 2018 – A Poem

Serenity was a long holiday weekend.
Me floating in my pool
You, off riding your bicycle

Quiet, stillness, lassitude
Relaxed in the giant float I bought on Amazon
Peace and tranquility
Summer and heat and happiness

Floating, floating, floating
Staring up at the blue sky
Leaves and squirrels rustling in the trees

Pure bliss

Alone, yet not lonely
Alive and aware of the beauty of the world

Floating, floating, relaxed and soothed
By the water's gentle lapping
By the sun's encouraging warmth

The perfect life…

Eyes closed now, taking in the sound of the birds,
The buzz of the insects,
The gentle movement of the leaves,
I hear the back door slam

Back from your ride: Honey, I'm home! What a great ride! What a beautiful day!

You come to the pool and feel the water and shudder at its coldness
And I float over to the edge
To you
And I ask about your ride, and we chat, and you say, I'm going to make dinner; don't stay in too long, you're getting burnt

And you give my float a push that propels me across the pool

Eyes closed now
Floating gently around the pool in the current you created
I enjoy listening to the sounds of your activity

The rustle as you unpack the groceries you bought
The water running as you clean the chicken
The door slightly squeaking as you step out on the deck to light the grill
The metallic-sounding slam as you shut the grill lid

The chair legs grinding across the wooden deck
You sitting down at the table with a loud groan as your weary bones settle after the long long bike ride
The chop chop chop as you cut up veggies and chicken
Rustling and movement and busy noises

And I know you are creating our delicious dinner
And I know in an hour or so you will bring out the wine

And I'll hear you uncork the bottle
And I'll hear the clink of the glasses

And this is serenity
This is our life
This is the world we created together
Life with you is

Pure bliss

And in a little while, you'll say, Honey, get out of the pool and join me for a drink. Dinner's almost ready.

And I'll say, Okay, I'll get out in a bit.

But let me float a few minutes more
Let me float in my pool, alone with my thoughts and serenity and the dreamy happiness of this

Perfect day…

In this perfect life…in the perfect house…with the perfect yard…

And the perfect husband

And now I float in the pool and I wait and I wait and I wait
But I will not hear the back door slam

And the silence is deafening
And the serenity is gone
And the sadness is overwhelming

No reason now for me to leave the giant float from Amazon
So I float and I float and I float
And I try to enjoy the perfect day
And I try to find reasons to go on in my perfect life …in my perfect house…with the perfect yard…

Without my perfect husband

And I tell myself the world is still full of life and sounds and serenity
But I daydream of you and memories of summer weekends we shared in the past

And I long to hear the sounds you made
And I strain to hear the back door slam
But all is quiet as I float float float

Alone in my pool

May 28, 2018

On Grief and Grandkids

When Rick died suddenly last August, my son Brandon and his wife Lindsey were forced to quickly research the best way to handle explaining his death to my then 2 ½-year-old grandson, Jonas. They didn't want to confuse him by telling him that his Papa "went away," because he might think Papa was coming back. They knew he was too young to fully understand the concept of death (I still have many questions, myself) so they simply told Jonas that Papa was sick, and then he died. They explained that we wouldn't be seeing him anymore, that he wouldn't be coming back.

Jonas seemed puzzled, then asked, "Did Boba die, too?" I'm Boba. For some unknown reason, Jonas started calling me that at a very young age. And Jonas knew that Papa and Boba were together all the time, so it was a natural question. They told him, no, Boba didn't die. They brought him to my house to see me a few days later, and warned me that he kept repeating, "Where's Papa? Papa died." In fact, when he first arrived, he went from room to room looking for his Papa and kept returning to me to ask over and over, "Where's Papa?" It broke my heart, but, as with everything else concerning Rick's death, I got used to it.

Rick and I have been blessed with five wonderful grandchildren, from ages 16 to just over one year. They have been a bright spot in my life and have helped me find joy in my grief as I struggle through holidays and birthday celebrations without him. The three older kids are each coping quietly with their "Tall Papa's" death. The baby was born a few months before Rick died. But Jonas is at the "why?" stage, and handling his many many questions about Rick can be daunting.

I babysit the youngest two once a week. Nearly every week following Rick's death, Jonas mentioned Papa. Often, he wanted to look at his photos on my phone. He would swipe through the pictures, then look up at me and say, "Papa died. Papa was sick." He'd look thoughtful for a minute or so, and then resume playing.

At first, I would quietly shed a few tears, but eventually, I was able to simply smile and agree. Week after week, at some point in my visit, Jonas would say, "Boba, Papa died." And I would say, "Yes, Jonas, he did." At one point, after saying, "Boba, Papa died," he laughed and said, "Papa was crazy!"

I have no idea why he said that, but perhaps he remembered his Papa acting goofy and telling him silly things when we visited. For whatever reason, he added the "crazy" part, and that little additional comment always makes me smile.

Nine months have passed. Jonas turned three at the end of December, and he's learning more about life and still questioning everything. At various times, he's asked me different and more difficult questions: Why

did Papa get sick? Why did Papa die? Where did Papa go? Why can't Papa come back?

I'm never sure how to answer in a way a three-year-old will understand, so I usually honestly answer, I don't know why, Jonas. Papa was sick. Papa died.

Earlier this year, he also experienced the fact that other Papas die, too.

My nephew-in-law's father died in February, and Jonas was at the funeral. Seeing his favorite cousins crying over their Papa in the casket confused him. Whose Papa is that? So many Papas dying! At one point in the following weeks, we had to correct him when he heard that Lindsey's dad (who lives in another state) was sick and he started telling people THAT Papa died, too. A Facetime visit helped to convince him that his Florida Papa was still alive.

Once, he saw a photo of my deceased father, and asked who he was. We explained that this was a picture of his daddy's Papa, and that he had also died. As a result of grasping that other Papas have also died, his comments about Rick have evolved a bit to clarify which Papa he means. A few months ago, he began saying, "Boba, Papa died, MY Papa died."

I know you're never prepared for what crazy notions a child will have, but the other night when I was sitting with the kids, Jonas threw me for a loop. Rick and I often stopped in our local park because we loved to work outdoors on our laptops, or have lunch, or just hang out. He bought us each a folding chair with a little fold-down side table that we kept in the car so we'd always be prepared for our impromptu park visits. I still carry one with me, just in case I feel like having some quiet time in our favorite spot.

Wednesday was a beautiful day, and Jonas wanted to play in his front yard while he waited for his parents to come home. I pulled the folding chair out of my car and sat in it while Jonas was running around. Always observant, Jonas ran over to me and said, "That's Papa's chair!" I responded that Papa had given it to me. He said, "Papa died. MY Papa died." I told him, yes, his Papa had died, and for no reason, I added, "Papa was my husband." Jonas said somberly, "Papa was MY husband, too."

As is often the case lately, I laughed and cried at the same time.

I'll admit, in the first months after Rick's death, it was difficult stemming the tears week after week when Jonas talked about his Papa being dead, but now, more often than not, it makes me smile that he still remembers his Papa so fondly. I know as time passes, he'll probably lose all memory of his Papa Rick, but when he's older, I'll be able to share old pictures of them together and tell him stories about his "crazy" Papa for years to come.

It's difficult explaining death to small children. It's tough enough coping with the questions myself. In the nine months following Rick's death, how many times have I pondered those same questions Jonas has: Why did Rick get sick? Why did Rick die? Where did he go? Will I see him again someday?

And I don't have any satisfactory answers. All I can tell myself is: Rick was sick. Rick died. Rick isn't coming back. But I'll always cling to the hope that I'll see him again someday.

May 31, 2018

Rick and Jonas two months before Rick's death

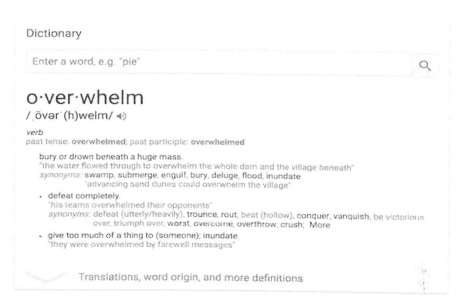

A Lifeline of Hope for the Newly Grieving: It Gets Better

As someone who has now survived nine months of widowhood, I decided to extend a lifeline of hope for anyone who's in the first few month of grieving. It's a surprising realization and something that occurred to me only this morning:

It gets better.

I never would have believed it in the early days – the days, weeks, and months after Rick died. The one word I can use to describe what I felt is **overwhelmed**: I was completely overwhelmed by sadness, stress, anxiety, grief, loneliness, dread, and hopelessness. I was emotionally devastated and was constantly plagued by an awful, indescribable, sick sensation. Every single thing around me reminded me:

He's gone. He's gone. He's gone.

Getting out of bed every morning was the most difficult thing I've ever done in my 61 years of life. Knowing that the act of waking in an empty bed would trigger pain that would be followed by millions of thoughts that caused more pain all day long, every day. Thoughts that ranged from fear that I would never be the same, fear that I could not continue my life without him, to anxiety at the desperate ALONENESS of it all. Anxiety because the house was too quiet, too strange. It was an eerie, empty existence in a house that had only a few short days earlier been our home.

How could I rise in the morning knowing that I would face fear, loneliness, and pain every hour of every day? How could I pretend to function around others when my thoughts were consumed by Rick? Memories of him alive, awareness that I had been in denial about how sick he was, focusing over and over on his last breath.

Then there was the constant regret, regret that I didn't do enough to save him. There must have been something I could have done. SOMETHING! I failed him. I didn't suggest a new doctor or a trial drug, or – most of all – I had caused his death because it was my idea that morning for him to bring in the garbage. He fell, he broke his hip, he died. Yes, I know logically that I didn't kill him. The cancer killed him. But there was no convincing me of that in the "early days" of overwhelming all-consuming grief.

And then, I had to try to continue to function in this empty, empty pain-filled world. I had to revisit everything we had ever done together by myself. I had to sleep in our bed, eat at our table, sit in our living room in the evenings…the quiet, quiet living room. Rick was a 6'5" 300-pound larger-than-life presence and his absence was a tangible entity in our home. His "non-presence" loomed everywhere.

I know every other widow and widower gets it. The utter confusion and pain at being one half of a couple that is no longer. Half of my soul had been ripped from my being. It may be trite, but those sad songs described it perfectly: my heart was broken in two. It literally ached. My spirit was shattered. I was overwhelmed that life was continuing on around me without Rick. Overwhelmed by the idea of living the rest of my life without him, when we had so many plans. We had our world. We had US.

It was as if the wind had been knocked out of me and I was left gasping for breath.

And so I existed for months, overwhelmed by grief and life and the idea of a future without Rick. My days were all the same. I awoke, I remembered, I cried. I forced myself to rise and go to work and activities, and all the while, I faked being a "normal" person. I chatted with others while trying to ignore the constant throbbing emotional pain. I lived through memory after all-consuming memory and continued to move forward, although I really had no urge to go on. My life was one big effort at distraction. Trying with little success to find something that interested me. Trying to keep busy and to find reason to continue with the life I had ahead of me, when I longed to curl up into a ball and lie in our bed under his favorite blanket, just replaying our life together over and over in my head. Trying to find hope, but overwhelmed by sadness.

Besides trying to cope with the idea of a solo future and the sudden change in my world, I was also overwhelmed by the constant pain of the good memories, the memories that made me miss him more each day. I heard "our" songs and remembered us dancing together on the deck in the moonlight. As I watched my Timehop and Facebook memories unfold each day and revisited what we had been doing on this same day in our history last year, and the year before that, and the one before that, I longed to return to those days and relive it all again. I passed places where we had shopped and streets we had driven together daily and the tears flowed as I drove. In the evenings, I returned home to an empty house, and sat for minutes, sometimes an hour in the car, trying to get the nerve to enter the silent house, knowing I wouldn't hear him bellow out a greeting when I opened the door.

At home, I expected him around every corner and was disappointed once again when I realized my loss. I remembered his jokes, his voice, his smell, his touch, his facial expressions, his sayings, his habits, his likes, and his dislikes, and I all I longed for was to see him and touch him again.

And every day was the same – oh sure, some were better than others, and some things that were difficult to cope with began to get a little better. The wailing with grief became mostly just sobbing. And then I could revisit places that used to make me sob but now only caused me to shed a few tears, but, in general, there was still that feeling of overwhelming sadness and none of my waking mornings brought much to look forward to.

In the spring, nearly eight months after his death, I did the unthinkable. I drove from Michigan to Florida – our yearly spring trek – without him. I revisited the gulf where we shared each sunset. I sat alone, still not quite believing that he wasn't in his usual spot next to me on the beach. I revisited the motels where we stayed, the places where we ate, all our favorite views and vistas. Alone.

It was the bravest thing I've ever done. And, again, only one word could describe it: it was quite simply, overwhelming. On the first evening I arrived, with my plan in place to visit that first sunset without him, I literally collapsed on the bed sobbing, frozen with fear and grief, unable to walk to the door. This was OUR PLACE, this was the last happy place we shared before the cancer stole him away. This was our favorite place on earth. I can't do it!

I tried to think of someone to call, but I knew I couldn't reach out to family or friends, because no one could "save" me. No one could bring him back, and that was the only thing that could make my world right again. I was on my own, and I had to continue this journey completely and utterly alone. So I went, and I cried, but then I felt him there! I knew he was encouraging me to go on. I knew he wanted me to have a life. And, suddenly, I knew that it would be painful, but it would all be okay.

I survived.

And now, two months later, and nine and a half months after his death, the thought hit me just this morning: I am no longer overwhelmed.

It didn't happen all at once, or overnight. I look back on the feelings and thoughts I've recorded in my blog, and I realize that month by month it's been getting a little easier. Little by little, the pain has been becoming more manageable. And it hasn't happened through my own efforts. About a month after Rick died, I began weekly appointments with a grief counselor. I also have family and friends that have supplied me with lots and lots of love and support. But, all the help in the world couldn't have relieved my suffering. Only time could heal this awful wound.

I still love him. I still miss him. I still feel married to him, and I still wear my ring. I still think about him daily (and on some days, hourly). But the pain is no longer constant, and when it hits hard, it's not AS hard as it once was. It's more often than not a "manageable" pain. And often, when I'm alone, I'm just alone and okay with it now. I'm not so much "half a person," as I am just simply a person on my own. Maybe that doesn't make sense to someone who hasn't lost a spouse, but I think you'll get what I mean.

And I guess that's what I want to tell you. You — who are in the early days or months after losing your spouse — although you probably won't believe me. You won't be able to picture ever not feeling the way you do now, but it will happen. One day, you'll realize that you awoke and just felt a mild sadness at being alone, not an all-out screaming, throbbing pain. And you'll no longer linger in your bed every morning, afraid to rise and feel the pain (although, it will still happen some days). You'll arise and go about your day feeling sad, and probably lonely, even when surrounded by others, but you won't feel that heart-rending pain, the kind that makes you want to stop whatever you're doing and wrap yourself in a blanket and wail.

You'll feel a little more like a person, and a little less like a half-empty soul. And you won't feel so overwhelmed. You'll be able to breathe.

Maybe you'll still not be "yourself," because face it, half of you is gone and you're still coping with that and probably will be for a long time. But maybe, just maybe, you'll know you've survived this far, and you'll be able to picture continuing on with your life.

You'll have a glimmer of hope. And even a glimmer is something.

June 4, 2018

Alone at the Crossroads

I feel like I'm at some weird crossroads in my life: the intersection of clinging to my life with Rick and forging on to my solo life ahead. My head is filled with conflicting thoughts. The pain, the grief has lessened (most days), and I've realized that by living without Rick for nearly ten months, I now feel more like an individual and less like a partner, a wife. And, although I feel some relief that I'm adapting to widowhood, that I'm moving forward, the idea that I no longer feel "as married" depresses me. It's just one more loss I've endured since Rick died.

I know I haven't truly been "a wife" since August 13, 2017. On that day, I became a widow. Yes, I know that, logically. But what's logic have to do with grief?

In July 1997, I chose to be Mrs. Richard Palmer. I chose to be his wife for life. And on that day, when I held his hand and stared into his eyes, I pledged to remain his wife for my entire life. As we exchanged our vows, I never considered that my vow would end with his life. I never dreamed that by saying "till death do us part," I put such a fine point on it. When I read somewhere that my "vows were fulfilled upon his death," that phrase made my heart hurt.

So, although it sometimes seems unbelievable, I've accepted the painful fact I'm a widow, not a wife. My counselor says that by writing through my pain, by not avoiding it or trying to ignore it, I've made remarkable progress. She said taking my solo journey back to our Florida vacation spot was a brave effort at closure that helped me realize I can travel and experience life alone. She says I'm adapting well to my new life alone and finding ways to fill the many voids left by Rick's death. While admitting I'll never be able to replace him and his loss, she says I've worked to fill many of the needs he fulfilled in my life socially and intellectually, and found ways to cope with the sheer number of things he did in our marriage that I now need to take care of myself, or hire others to do for me. I've done well adapting to my "new normal."

To have and to hold from this day forward, for better, for worse, for richer, for poorer in sickness and in health, to love and to cherish, till death us do part

I guess I've earned an "A" in grieving.

Emotionally, some days I see daylight, but some nights are still awful. Sometimes the storm hits and I am back at day one, back at the hospital desperately hoping that I'll have another twenty years to fulfill those vows. Often times, I resist this forward motion, and sob my way through the memories, angry that life moved so quickly, mourning the fleeting time we enjoyed. I long to be back in my happy married life, back with my larger-than-life Rick. I resist any forward movement. I don't want it to be over.

I want time to stand still, because every second means Rick and our life together moves farther into the past, deeper into my memory. Wrong or not, unhealthy or not, in a way, sometimes I still want Rick to BE my life – more than he was when he was alive.

So I stand at this crossroads, feeling ready to move forward, but resisting change, resisting movement, resisting progress, resisting putting my past behind me, resisting losing any more of my "Rickworld" than I have to. And apparently, that's my next step in grieving process:

To find an enduring connection with the deceased while embarking on a new life.

I know grief can't really be neatly dissected and categorized and described like line items on a bill of goods, but as I delve into the "grief process," I do see some patterns that my own grieving has followed. The steps defined by J. William Worden have seemed to fit my pattern (although I usually take two steps forward, one step back, and I can be at step one again in the blink of an eye).

Worden proposed these four tasks of grief:

Task 1: Accept the reality of the loss.
Task 2: Process your grief and pain.
Task 3: Adjust to the world without your loved one in it.
Task 4: Find a way to maintain a connection to the person who died while embarking on your own life.

So, how neatly does that fit? Task 4 truly describes my crossroads. Diligent student of life — and now grief — that I am, I'll seek out more information and advice on this step. Although I do feel a glimmer of interest in the "embarking on my own life" part of the task, right now, I'm more focused on finding the way to maintain a connection to Rick. As time moves on so quickly, the pain of separation worsens – he's been gone so long! It's nearing ten months since I've seen him and held him and talked to him. How can that be?

It's an awkward position straddling that crossroads: one foot firmly stuck on the road to the past and one foot positioned on the road towards my new solo journey. I will work to find ways to maintain all the beautiful memories, the feeling that he's here with me, his voice in my head, his love in my heart, before I can move both feet forward. I'll strive to find that way to move forward, while I still long so much for the past. I desperately need to maintain my connection to Rick while embarking on my new life without him.

June 8, 2018
Four tasks from *Grief Counseling and Grief Therapy, Fourth Edition: A Handbook for the Mental Health Practitioner*, by J. William Worden. Springer Publishing Company; 4 edition (August 11, 2008)

See You on the Other Side

I was running late this morning (nothing new about that). But today I was particularly late, and at the time I got in my car and started it up, I'm usually already sitting at my desk at work. I wouldn't normally have been in the car when this song was playing.

Timing is everything.

So I started my car, and my radio was on and set to the Sirius Coffee House station, the station that plays a lot of acoustic music. A new song was playing, a song I had never heard before. It was called, "See You on the Other Side."

Look up the lyrics some time. Every word seemed like a message from Rick to me. Let the waterworks begin!

I sat in my running car in the driveway, unable to put the car in gear. At first I thought, no no no! Please, I don't want to start crying now. I have to get to work. I don't have time to cry.

I was okay this morning. I woke up fine and ran around getting ready for work without crying once. I was handling my new normal. I was having an uneventful morning. The reason I'm running late is because it was difficult to get up at 7 after staying up until 1 am looking at old photos of Rick – and finally crying myself to sleep at 2am. Please please please, don't make me start again now.

But, instead of changing the station and backing out of my driveway, I gave in to the inevitable and stayed where I was and listened to the rest of the song. And after it was through, I changed my viewpoint to, "Thank you."

Thank you, Rick, for the message. I love you too, honey. And I sobbed, but I felt peace, because I could hear him talking to me through the lyrics, words that spoke to me so eloquently about the status of our marriage – and our love – when he died last year.

But in our limb of bone and lace
And time and love and body aches
I loved you more
I loved you more
But a clock keeps ticking down…

He was 63 and I was 60. And although I feel cheated that we didn't have more time, we had definitely arrived at the time of "love and body aches" and I know he loved me more than when we met 21 years earlier. Our marriage had grown from the initial "wild love and insatiable sex" part when we met, to a place of quiet love and comfort, "of time and love and body aches." And, yes, I know he loved me more at the end, as only two people who have shared 20+ years of births and deaths, happiness and grief, and all the joys and sufferings of real life can love each other.

And in our years together, Rick treated me like a queen. He loved doing sweet little tasks for me. He enjoyed buying me trinkets and little surprises all the time, so I can almost hear him jokingly singing these lyrics about him spending his life in "…Your Majesty's service…"

So, yes, when I first heard the words of this song, I was upset and disappointed because I didn't want to be reminded of my grief. I was happy that more often than not lately I'm waking up without all those strong emotions. I needed to be calm and steady so I could go about my day, to put away the feelings of loss because I didn't have time for grief this morning.

But after the first shock of hearing those poignant and personal lyrics, after taking time to give in and listen to the rest of the song, I'm thankful I was running late. I'm thankful, despite the tears, that I was in my car at just the right time to hear this song, because – crazy as it sounds – I know this was a message from Rick, and I'm happy to have received it.

The song reminds me of all we shared, of how much we loved each other, and that even though he's gone physically, he's not gone from my memories or my heart. He'll never really be gone, will he?

And, yes, I'm a crazy widow who's looking for signs from Rick everywhere, but I don't care if I am crazy. Rick's love for me was embodied in these lyrics. And I have a message for Rick:

I want you to know that I'll love you all my days, and when I close my eyes on this lifetime, I'll see you on the other side. Yes, honey, I'll see you on the other side

June 12, 2018

> The world is very quiet
> without you around.
>
> – Lemony Snicket

The Sounds of Silence

I miss the sounds of Rick.

I never thought of myself as an "auditory" person. I've always been more visual: I love the written word; I love looking at photographs and art. Yes, I've always put music on the top of my list of things that I enjoy, but I never realized until Rick died how much I enjoyed "the sounds" of living with him, the comfort of hearing him in another room, going about his tasks.

Our house – my life – is so quiet now, and one of the most difficult and unexpected things I've had to cope with in this grieving process is getting used to the quiet, the deafening quiet.

As most couples do, Rick and I often shared odd little details about our lives, our histories, our likes and dislikes. Once, when we were lying in each others arms during one of our favorite Saturday afternoon naps, just chatting about nothing, he told me that as a boy, he used to find comfort listening to his mother talk on the phone in the other room. He said it was soothing to listen to her voice drone on as he lay on his bed reading. I understood that, and can still conjure up memories of a summer Sunday afternoon as a young girl, up in my bedroom, listening to the background noise of the baseball game on the TV in the living room below. I could hear my dad clatter and clang pans as he cooked our Sunday afternoon dinner (chicken and "stuffings," as we called them). I recall the sounds of the muted conversations of my mom and dad as they chatted below.

Those were comforting sounds from my youth, but until Rick talked about his, I had never thought to give voice to those elusive memories. He had often expressed his enjoyment at listening to a storm outside our bedroom window, or to the sounds of summer as he lay in bed reading a book, or lay down for a nap – people mowing lawns, kids playing, cars driving by – but again, I hadn't realized how much I loved those comforting sounds, as well.

Rick was a writer – and I always enjoyed the poetic way he had of describing his childhood memories – or just about anything from his past. He'd obviously paid attention to every detail of his surroundings, and his vivid descriptions brought his memories to life. And, most often, he recounted those stories by describing the sounds, as well as the scenes.

And now that he's gone, I realize that two decades of "his noises" in our home were very much a part of my life. The absence of those sounds can strike me with agony when I least expect it. So, I've come to realize that grieving also encompasses coming to terms with the auditory losses. Not only can love songs, and old photos, and the sight of articles of his clothing or other items he owned trigger grief, the "sounds of silence" in our home can, as well.

Rick was a huge, loud, viable presence in our home, and living with him was not a quiet life.

Sunday mornings, I often awoke to hearing him rattling pots and pans as my father used to, preparing something for the slow cooker, or starting our breakfast. Sunday afternoons, hearing the French door to the yard slam over and over throughout the day, as he went in and out, working on a project in the yard.

The lawn mower, the Paul Simon music, the rapid typing as his large fingers clattered over a keyboard in a remarkably fast pace for a "hunt and peck" typist, were all typical daily sounds that are missing from my life now.

I miss the groans he emitted as he arose from his chair or sat down again – or as he loudly clomped up the basement stairs after getting a can of something from the larder. I miss hearing the deep timber of his voice as he called the cat "Dumbhead" when she sat staring into the yard after he'd opened the door for her to go outside for the umpteenth time that day. I miss him calling out for me to find something he was looking for (that was usually in a very obvious place). I miss the sound of him singing along to his favorite songs while he played air guitar, or swearing when something didn't work correctly on his computer, or mumbling to himself as he tried to fix something. I miss the sound of him banging cupboard doors and dropping things. And – most of all – I miss the sound of him snoring softly next to me in bed at night.

I miss the sounds of life – our life.

Oh, I'm getting used to it, as I am to just about everything that has changed since his death. In the first months after he died, I used to avoid being home most evenings because the silence was so awful, but, after ten months of enduring his absence, I can cope with coming home to the empty house. Fridays working at home, Saturdays and Sundays in the quiet, quiet house were severely depressing, but now, it's just the way it is.

But some afternoons, like today, the silence is palpable, and I'll sit here in the quiet remembering with fondness how noisy my life with Rick used to be. I'll close my eyes and search for those auditory memories. I'll pretend to myself that he's still in his office typing away, or outside puttering around. And, if I try hard enough, I'll hear him again – my loud, boisterous, larger-than-life man – and life will be back to normal.

June 18, 2018

The Last Spray Bottle

I was tidying up the kitchen yesterday, and I reached for the spray bottle of cleaner. I noticed it's almost empty and reminded myself that I need to add it to my shopping list. Then my mind started its typical chain of thoughts... Rick bought this bottle. He bought a couple of bottles at the same time and this is the last bottle... It's the last bottle Rick bought... And it's nearly gone.

So, of course, I started to cry. Why? Because it's one more "last" thing, one more reminder that at some point, there will be nothing left of him here, no item he touched. Eventually, every small insignificant item that he purchased will be used up, emptied, and discarded, like the old frozen meat I found last month in the back of my freezer, or the outdated ketchup in the door of the fridge.

Rick's been gone more than ten months, almost a year now. That in itself is difficult to comprehend. He was just here, wasn't he? We were just together, happy, blissfully unaware of what was ahead. Weren't we?

No, finding outdated food and coming across nearly used up cleaning supplies reminds me that he's been gone a long while. And it's been even longer since the "normal" time when he did all the shopping and fetching, because in the last months before he died, he was sick or weak or enduring medical treatments, and not up to shopping.

Rick LOVED to shop – even grocery shop. I never understood the appeal, but I relished the fact that he did, and reveled in the luxury of never having to step foot in a grocery store because of him. And this bottle of spray cleaner at one point had absolutely no significance in my life. It was just one of many things Rick bought on his numerous shopping trips each week.

Until now, months after his death, when realizing the cleaner is nearly empty is somehow a significant emotional trigger. These days, more than a year since he was healthy enough to shop, finding an outdated food item in the bottom of a cupboard can transport my mind back to when life was normal. Finding an old can of bouillon he bought to use in his favorite chicken soup recipe – or the expired can of diced tomatoes he put into his "secret" marinara sauce – conjures up the smells and sounds of him cooking, brings back the memory of our simple, happy life together, and reminds me how long it's been since those days were here.

But thinking about this particular spray bottle of cleaner also makes me realize the more complicated part of these memories, and that is WHAT I choose to remember. Each once-insignificant item can generate thoughts that encompass an entire history surrounding its origins, and sometimes provokes memories I'd rather leave forgotten.

Take the spray bottle…Rick purchased this particular brand because I was so disgusted with the type he had bought before. He bought a spray cleaner with bleach to use in our kitchen. And the bleach got on my clothes when I used it to perform a quick kitchen counter clean up. And I bitched about it, but he didn't think my complaints were important and, besides, he liked the cleaner with bleach. So I bitched some more, and he eventually bought another brand – this one – and what's left in this last bottle is all that remains.

And, of course, this triggers the regrets…why did I complain about such stupid things? Why didn't I just throw my arms around him and thank him for all that he did? He bought the damned groceries and spray cleaner in the first place – and then I had the nerve to complain! Why did I cause him one moment of upset? Why wasn't I kinder to him? Why didn't I appreciate the millions of things he did for me? Why did I argue with him about something so petty?
What kind of wife was I?

A human one.

A human wife, with human foibles who is now a widow who regrets nearly every poor decision, complaint, lack of appreciation, harsh word, and moment not spent with the man I now miss with an agonizing intensity. A human wife who couldn't see or imagine a future without this husband who cherished and loved me and did small acts of kindness for me many times every day.

So now, I battle with myself every time I come across these small "last" items, these insignificant grief triggers. I try to ignore the bad memories, the regrets, the parts I can't go back and change. I loved him with all my heart, and he knew it. Didn't I thank him for shopping all the time? Didn't I perform a million small acts of kindness for him, as well? Didn't I rub his back, praise his deeds, tell him how proud I was of his talents, thank him for small favors?

Yes, I did. And I'll struggle to remember those loving acts instead of vilifying myself for every small transgression. He knew I loved him. I told him, held him, kissed him, praised him, and did anything I could to prove that throughout our marriage, and then I told him, loved him, held him, and kissed him at his bedside, until he took his last breath. I wasn't perfect. I was human, and so was he.

And now that he's gone, I need to focus on remembering the wonderful life we shared, and stop the nagging thoughts about those petty misunderstandings from intruding and ruining those glorious memories.

Dealing with grief and triggered memories is a complicated thing. There are so many things I can't control. I can't stop life's forward motion. I can't change the fact that the man I love is gone, or that I'm left in our home alone, with a million reminders that, day by day, my life with Rick continues to recede more into the past. I also can't change anything I regret from those times we shared. I don't have any choice about so much that occurs in my life, but I can choose to focus on the caring memories and the kind deeds, to reminisce about the thousand precious little loving things we did to show one another how much we cared.

So maybe I won't focus on the argument about the spray cleaner, or the fact that Rick won't be around to purchase the next bottle. Maybe I'll remember how much I loved the man who did all our shopping and appreciate all the times he brought me little gifts and trinkets from those numerous shopping trips.

As I use the cleaner on the countertop, maybe I'll think about how we enjoyed working together installing that counter on the new kitchen island when we remodeled the house. Or remember how important it was to Rick to build the spacious island in the middle of the kitchen so he'd have plenty of room to roll out the dough for pizza crust, and how we meticulously measured and planned the cupboard arrangement and labored together to assemble it.

Or perhaps I'll envision the production he made every Friday "pizza night." Our favorite music playing in the background, me sitting on the stool next to the island… I loved to watch him roll out the dough with his huge, massive hands before spreading on some of that home-made marinara sauce, adding spices and lots of mozzarella cheese, and then inviting me to choose from the piles of toppings he'd laid out for my selection: pepperoni, chopped ham, diced onions, mushrooms, green peppers, jalapeños, and cilantro. And afterwards, after the pizza had been eaten and the wine had been drunk out on the back deck, and it was nearly time for bed, I'd use that bottle of spray cleaner to clean up the food splatters while Rick wrapped up the leftovers at the end of another enjoyable evening spent together.

So maybe I'll remind myself not to focus on the last nearly empty spray bottle or the argument that led to him buying it. There are a million wonderful memories from my life with Rick that can bring me a smile, so maybe, just maybe, I'll choose one of those instead.

June 25, 2018

You'll always be with me, like a handprint on my heart

The Handprint on the Wall

As widowed life becomes "normal," not every morning is horrible anymore. It used to be – a few short months ago – that the bravest thing I've ever done was to get out of bed in the morning and face the day ahead.

In the first month or two after Rick died, I was in some type of fugue state. I lived, breathed, moved, and even returned to work two weeks after he died, but looking back, I realize I wasn't really there. My body and brain may have been functioning, and I appeared to be alive, but I wasn't. I was in a place with Rick, some limbo in my mind, where we could stay together a little longer before I had to face the fact that he had to leave me for good.

Partly because of the fog of grief, partly because of a small daily dose of Xanax, it was like I was drifting on a cloud, a horrible black cloud, but all the while, I performed my duties and interacted with the living world.

In that "between" land – between my life and his death – my mind drifted back and forth between the feeling of still being connected to my living, breathing, husband, and the reality of being a lone survivor.

I knew I was still alive, and that life requires decisions, communication, interaction with others, and mental effort, so I tried my best to move forward, but my thoughts were still centered around "us." We, we, we… we did this, we did that. He and I loved this; Rick and I always did that. He was still part of me, very very very much part of me. We were still one. It was almost like he was my shadow, unseen, but still present with me everywhere. I was consumed with the physical loss of someone with whom I had shared every aspect of my being, and kept him very much alive in my mind.

As time went on, I started to become "normal" again, and that was when I had to come to terms with the fact that he was really gone, and I was really alone – and being more conscious of that hurt like hell. As the fog began to lift, the pain upon rising each morning worsened. But I had to live, and I had to work, and I had to rise, so I did.

I have had a fortunate life, a healthy life, and I've never experienced the kind of physical or mental pain some people endure every day, constant pain due to physical afflictions: rheumatoid arthritis, neuralgia, fibromyalgia, and other painful conditions, or mental afflictions, such as bipolar disorders or depression. No, I may feel a twinge or two of arthritis pain every now and then, and I've been pretty sick a few times, but I've never had to conquer pain as a daily challenge when I get out of bed each morning – until Rick's death, when grieving his loss caused an emotional and constant pain that began upon rising and didn't abate until I was finally able to fall asleep at the end of a very long, horrible day.

In the past couple of months, that pain has subsided quite a bit. I expect that something will probably trigger a meltdown or two each day, but the tears don't flow for quite as long, and I am in control of my thoughts most of the time now. Because I feel so much more in control, more "normal," the grief triggers come as more of a surprise, but I've accepted the reality: Rick is dead and I am not. I still feel a connection, but it's dwindling – which in itself is a painful realization. In all honesty, I'm not sure I want to accept that my life has gone on, because being with him was everything I've ever wanted my life to be.

So, today, I arose, and it was a "new normal" morning: Yup, Rick is still dead – acknowledged and accepted – now time to get ready for work.

I grabbed my robe and headed for the shower. Once in the tub, I had finished lathering and rinsing my hair, and I turned to face the shower spray. I happened to glance up, and I noticed something I hadn't in the past ten months since Rick's been gone. There, against the white tile, was a faint, shadowy handprint. A large handprint. Rick's handprint.

For some reason, this was a punch to my gut. Besides a commentary on my cleaning skills (or lack of), it stunned me to see it. Just when I fear that he's fading from my life, that all evidence of him will soon be gone from our home, I see this? My larger-than-life husband's larger-than-life handprint at nearly the ceiling level of our shower?

And, wow, did it take me back. My mind spiraled back to the many times I watched him shower in our 21 years together. I had an acute vision of all six foot, five inches of him, covered in suds from the top of his large bald head to his size 14W feet, and he was a sight to behold. At my "normal" height, I had never in my life had a problem with the position of a showerhead on a wall, but Rick, of course, needed one that was a foot higher than most, if he wanted to shower comfortably (and not just rinse himself from mid-chest or below).

But, whatever the height of the shower head, he'd always have to duck to rinse the top of his head. And while doing so, he'd brace himself using one hand against the very top of the wall in front of him – at nearly ceiling level – before lowering his head under the water's spray, and using his other giant paw to sluice the water back and forth over the top of his head, then down across his face, from forehead to chin (all while emitting a loud, pleasurable sigh).

As I stared at the handprint, and envisioned the probability of how it got there, the memory brought me both pleasure and pain. One minute I was showering, the next, tears mingled with the spray of the shower on my face. I could picture him vividly, and it hurt to be reminded once more that I'd never see or touch that large soapy body again.

When the tears had subsided, I began to study the handprint. Yup, I'm positive it's in the exact location where his hand would have rested. I'm not even sure what the handprint is made of – I think that part of the wall – where wall meets ceiling – is dusty and the print from his wet hand left a clean spot. I know I never reach that high when cleaning the shower, because only the lower tiles have soap scum. So, here it is, like an archaeological artifact – proof that my husband existed. I almost wish I could preserve it somehow. Seal it in paraffin? Make a cement cast? Remove the tiles and frame them under glass?

No, crazy widow, no. At some point, you're going to have to wash that spot, just as you laundered the sheets and the pillow cases he last slept upon. Just as you discarded the expired food he bought and performed all the other updates and changes you were forced to make since he's been gone.

Of course, if I think about it, even though I've given away his shoes and coats, and tossed out his underwear and socks, I still haven't gotten rid of the rest of his clothing: his Hawaiian print shirts and superhero t-shirts still hang in his closet. And his last box of sugar-free Altoids is still sitting behind the lamp on the living room table where he left it. I also haven't touched the things on his nightstand, and a layer of dust is evidence of how long it's been since he read that book or drank from the empty Gatorade bottle.

So, maybe the handprint can remain on the wall, just a bit longer, until one day in the future, when I'm finally ready to wipe it away. Maybe I'm not quite "normal" yet, after all.

June 28, 2018

A Year's Worth of Dust and Memories

Dear Rick,

It's been nearly a year since you died. Does that mean I should be getting over the grief by now? Should I be capable of moving on in my "new" life without you?

In antiquated terms, is it almost time for me to remove my widow's weeds?

Almost a year…it will be eleven months next week. Remember when a year used to be a really long time? When we were children, a year was an interminable amount of time to wait for something: a year until the next birthday, a year until Christmas or until summer vacation would come around again.

As we matured, we were always surprised by how quickly time seemed to fly. Wow, we'd say. Do you believe that was a year ago? Each year seemed to fly by. And that's how I feel now, a strange dichotomy: this past year often seemed to be an interminable amount of time, a time filled with grief and sadness and missing you and adapting to your loss. It seemed such an awfully long time since I had seen you or touched you. Yet, at times, it seems like you were just here, as if – in a blink of an eye – you were here yesterday and suddenly disappeared. I can vividly picture some conversation we had, or some scene in my mind where you and I were doing some inane thing together, and it seems like the time between then and now flew by in an instant.

I know a year is a significant marker in all the advice given to those who grieve the loss of a significant loved one. My grief counselor is among many who warned me to wait one year after your death before making any major decisions about where to live, or about retiring from my job, or signing contracts, or remodeling, or any other drastic life changes. The newly grieving widow is too wrapped up in her grief and too emotional to think rationally. It's impossible to know what she really wants in that time of upheaval during the first 365 days after her husband's death. And throughout the year since you died, my thinking about what I want to do in the future and how I want to reshape my life now that you are no longer a part of it has changed and changed, and changed some more.

In the first weeks after you died, I thought, I will never leave here. This is the house we built together. Every part of our home has your imprint on it, your wants, your desires. You and I chose the wall colors, selected and laid the flooring, chose the kitchen cabinets and countertops and layout, and remodeled the kitchen by hand. You hand built the decks and landscaped the yard. We erected the gazebo last spring, in the last month when you felt well, before the cancer and side effects of the treatments tore at your body and weakened you until you could barely walk and could hardly stand. How could I ever leave the outdoor paradise you built for us, filled with memories as it is?

In the next few months, I thought, maybe I should downsize. I have to be practical. Rick is gone, and I need to move on. If I sold the house, and moved to one of those condos we viewed together, I could save money and I could retire sooner. I could begin some "new life," as vague as that idea is to me. I can live wherever I want, and do whatever I'd like – yet it's still difficult to come to terms with the idea that you and I won't be enjoying that future together. Our plans for retirement together are still stuck in my head. I'm struggling to decide what I want to do with my future now that you won't be part of it.

Then I realized that – for right now – I need to keep working because being without a schedule or the responsibilities of my job will leave me too much time to think. And, besides, I don't like the idea of condo living. I like my private yard. But, then again, the house and yard are so quiet now. Can I stand living here without you?

And you know what? All those thoughts and ideas swirling around in my head made me realize that nearly a year after you're gone, I still don't know what I want. It's still too soon to make a move. My emotions are still fragile. One minute, I think I'm coping and ready to "move on," the next, I'm shaking my head in shock that you really are gone and that I'll never see you again.

So, if the first year is the measure upon which to judge when the widow is too emotional to make important decisions, does it stand to reason that I'll be rational and unemotional – or more practical – after the one-year mark? Does that mean some time after August 13th of this year – your one year "angelversary" as they call it – that I will be able to think rationally again? Will I be less emotional about your death one month from now? Will I have come to terms with losing you? Will I know how I want to proceed as a "single person" once again?

If only that were true.

Yes, I've encountered and survived nearly every milestone anniversary without you now – first holiday (Labor Day), first Thanksgiving, my first birthday alone, first Christmas, New Year's Eve and one of the most awful feelings – beginning an entirely new year without you in it. I survived my first lone drive to our Florida paradise, the first spring and summer without you enjoying our pool and yard and barbecue, and the first Father's Day without you here. In that time, there have also been birthdays and other family celebrations where your absence was palpable. And they've all come and gone, and I've survived them all, some better than others.

There are only two more major "firsts" left to endure. Our anniversary next week, and the first anniversary of your death next month. Last July 12th, we were supposed to be celebrating our 20th anniversary, but your illness intruded on that, and it was pretty awful.

By last July, you couldn't remember how to send a text message, and sometimes would suddenly talk nonsense. And the doctors were puzzled at why you continued to decline. You were weak and had just survived the blood clots in your lung, but had lost 60 pounds and tried so damn hard to get up and walk every day. I never saw a man work harder to survive, and it was the most difficult thing I've had to watch: the very large, very vibrant man I loved suffering, and ultimately, succumbing to cancer. I also never knew what each day would bring. You were confused and sometimes incoherent – yet at other times, you were fine. It was like living with my dad when the Alzheimer's hit. I never knew if you were going to be "there" or not. So this July 12th really won't be the first wedding anniversary we didn't truly celebrate, but it will be the first without hope that we ever will again.

And, oddly, those "significant" expected milestones weren't the most difficult to endure. It was those "small firsts" – first night (or months) in our bed alone, first workday without you texting to say you were outside waiting to take me to lunch, or drive me home at the end of the day. First breakfast at our diner alone, first visit to the Home Depot, first time watching our favorite TV shows without you next to me enjoying them and commenting (ha! Kate McKinnon can imitate anyone! Or Rachel Maddow is really fired up tonight), first Avengers movie without you explaining who the minor characters were and their entire histories, first time I cooked your favorite chicken and veggies on the grill, every first time I heard one of "our songs," without you there to dance with me.

All those firsts – survived and conquered! It should be easy after all that, right? The year of firsts is almost over.

Yes, time has allowed some healing. I do feel more rational than I did a year ago. I still think about you daily, but not every hour of every day. Last Sunday brought another "small" – and admittedly odd – milestone event. I finally mustered up the courage to dust your bedside table for the first time since you've been gone. I picked up the empty Gatorade bottle that lay on its side since your last morning at home – the morning you fell in our driveway and the ambulance carted you off with a broken hip. I put your book in the drawer of the night stand. I removed the half empty Spiderman squirt bottle I had given you in an attempt to cheer you up right before you died. I swept the pocket change off the table top – the change you so casually tossed there one evening when you emptied your pockets before bed.

Yes, last Sunday, I removed my little bedside shrine to you and dusted the newly cleared surface because I was leaving for vacation and the house sitters shouldn't be subjected to nearly a year's worth of dust as they slept. It was a practical concern, and I needed to do it. And of course, I also had to take a little time before I started driving up north to cry over one more little loss, one more step towards leaving you behind.

A year of conquered firsts. A year's worth of dust and memories. I wonder if that's enough time to get over losing you? I think we both know the answer to that, don't we?

July 5, 2018

Time on My Hands

It's tough to go on vacations now…too much time to think. I'm up north at the family cottage for two weeks, and the weather is beautiful. I have nothing to do but bask in the sun, play with the grandkids on the sandy beach of Lake Huron, enjoy time with my family, and take in the beauty of these natural surroundings.

I also have plenty of time on my hands, time to think and reflect on the past. And, as I would expect, this vacation brings up memories of vacations past, and the bittersweet joy and sorrow that accompanies each remembrance.

Last night, alone in my tent at the end of a long, pleasurable day, I lay back on my inflatable bed and my mind immediately took me back to the two of us sleeping in a tent on this very beach twenty plus years ago. We arrived late, so we pitched the tent at night and didn't realize we had put it right over a little stream caused by the creek diverting towards the house. When we ducked inside the dark tent, we got drenched! It was hardly the romantic evening we had planned, but it was an unforgettable memory and we laughed about it for years.

That seems like a long long time ago, a distant memory from our first year together. But then earlier today, I was down on the beach staring out across the lake, feeling the sand beneath my bare feet, and – in an instant – I was transported back to the gulf in Florida. I'm watching you get ready to go down to the beach. The SUV hatch is open, and you're sitting on the back edge of the car, taking off your socks, putting on your beach shoes. I'm waiting impatiently, longing to get to the beach to watch the sunset, to get to our favorite place to sit and drink wine, so I can share one more memorable evening with you.

This memory doesn't seem that long ago. In fact, it seems like yesterday. I can almost touch you, you seem so close in my mind. But it wasn't yesterday. It was more than a year ago, our last vacation together in April 2017. We were on the vacation that was so bittersweet because deep down I feared it would be our last, but couldn't bear to think about it.

I remember that part vividly, too. I can feel the pain of living each day with your impending death looming over us. The doctor had just pronounced the cancer in remission, but said there was a 90 percent chance that it would return within the year. When we left his office, already packed and ready for our trip, you said that it was unbelievable how anticlimactic, how surreal it was. We were waiting and hoping for the good news that the chemo and radiation had killed the cancer cells, that you were in remission. We had already been informed in secret by a nurse the day before, and were so looking forward to the "official" news from the oncologist. So, yes, he told us the official excellent verdict – you were in remission. BUT…..it will be back. With small cell lung cancer, it's never truly "gone." It's lying dormant, and it will return, and there is no known treatment that works when it does. He pronounced that ominous news without a shred of doubt. Well…he hesitated a bit, and tossed us a bit of hope: you could be in the lucky 10 percent of those whose cancer didn't return.

And so we left town, neither of us knowing how to feel about that. We wanted to believe the best. We wanted to retain that tiny glimmer of hope. But sitting across from you in Florida, relaxing and holding hands in our beach chairs, I remember looking at you and trying to memorize your face. Looking at you and thinking, next year, he's not going to be here…drink him in, drink him in. Live in this moment. Love him while you can.

I was mourning the loss of you in advance. I've since learned this is called anticipatory mourning. I was already mourning all that I would lose if – when – I lost you. Yet I tried my damnedest to hope. Hope fought with logic for the ten months after your diagnosis. Hope fought with fear. Hope fought with sadness. Hope lost.

All these very real memories of those sunsets seem like yesterday, and I wonder now, how can this be? How can it be that our last trip to Florida was more than a year ago? How can it be that I'm nearing the one year anniversary of your death? You were just here. We were just talking and kissing and loving one another – and hoping – hoping we'd have many more years to do the same.

But no, it's over. It's more than a year since our trip to Florida, and I'm here on vacation in northern Michigan, alone in my tent overlooking the lake. And I have lots of time to remember, too much time to think. And so often this week, I find myself reaching back, back, back to you. And

you? You're slipping away from me, receding deeper into my past, to a time that's longer ago than I can believe possible.

Yes, I know I am blessed to have this place to come to. I'm fortunate to have a family and friends who love and support me. I'm luckier than many to have found you – the love of a lifetime – and make thousands of glorious memories in the twenty one years we were together. I'm even appreciative of every second of that ten months after the cancer diagnosis because life reminded us both very painfully, as life often does, that you wouldn't be here forever, that we are all mortal.

A cancer diagnosis reminded us to savor the time we had left, to live every single moment IN that moment, to seek out the sunsets on the beach, to eat the ice cream cones at 10 p.m. at McDonald's, to enjoy lunch in the park, to take long naps in each others' arms – to love each other desperately and completely in the last months of your life.

And now, as I continue on without you, and I enjoy my relaxing vacation at the cottage, I'm trying to live in the moment, because I've learned not to take life for granted. I'm trying my hardest to live my life to the fullest on my own. And – for my own sanity – I'm trying like hell to stay busy so I can avoid having too much time on my hands, too much time to think, too much time to grieve all that I've lost.

But I also know how lucky I am to have those thousand wonderful memories of our time together, all the love we shared in the time between the first year up here in a soggy tent on the beach and our last vacation on the gulf in the final months of your life. I have years and years of memories to cherish and relive and look back on.

Those visions of the past usually come to me unbidden, triggered by being in a familiar location, or the feeling of sand between my toes, hearing a song we used to dance to, or seeing a photo from our past. But I can also call upon any favorite memory in these quiet times, times when I have too much time to think, and I'm aware that having a lifetime of memories of times shared with the man I loved is a very very fortunate thing.

July 8, 2018

I Met a Man – A Poem

I met a man who loved the sun,
I knew at once he was the one.
He said, *I'll take you far and wide,*
If only you will be my bride.

I said "I do," sealed with a kiss,
And we began our wedded bliss.
His word was true, and we did go
Around the country to and fro.

He loved to wander and explore.
We drove for miles, then drove some more.
We saw the US, east to west.
(The beaches we both loved the best.)

From north to south we saw the sights:
Seattle mornings, Texas nights,
From Tijuana to South Dakota,
And down from Maine to Sarasota.

We swam nude beaches, drank fine wine,
Ate fresh lobster, drank moonshine.
From posh resort to cheap motel
(We saw things that I'll never tell.)

He took me to the Cornwall coast
(The trip I think I loved the most),
So I could search my history.
He even toured graveyards with me!

The London tube, Parisian wine,
Luxembourg, Belgium, and the Rhine,
And Amsterdam we went to twice,
To tour canals and ride the bikes.

We saw the sights, we swam the sea,
The road our favorite place to be.
We never knew what we'd discover
On those adventures with my lover.

And so we roamed for years together
Until we hit some stormy weather:
The doctors said his time is through
He's sick and he'll be leaving you.

So one last time we hit the road
Down to a sunny beach abode.
We drove until we reached the shore
So we could swim and play once more.

And four months later he was gone,
And I was left to travel on,
To visit places on my own –
To see those places all alone.

I said, I'm through, I can't go on.
My life is over. I'm all done.
Without my love, the fun is over;
I have no life without my lover.

I shut myself inside my home
No more would I go out to roam.
My love is gone, my love has died,
I need him traveling by my side.

But then I heard a little voice
That said, *My love you have no choice.*
I may be gone, but you're still here,
And life is precious – live, my dear.

I didn't choose to marry you
So you would quit when I was through.
So many places left to see
I want you to live life for me.

Next spring I knew what I must do.
(I knew that he would want me to.)
I got into my car one day,
And drove alone a long, long way.

I went back to our favorite spot:
The sunny beach we loved a lot.
And on the road, I felt him there.
I heard him whisper in my ear...

Go live your life; there's more to see.
Wherever you go, I will be.
We'll keep on traveling together.
My spirit's in your heart, forever.

To Rick, my happy wanderer. You loved me completely and showed me the world.
– All my love, Gerry

July 9, 2018

Happy Anniversary to Me

I thought it may all be past me now, the feeling of devastation, the tsunami of pain. Apparently, it wasn't.

I made it through our anniversary yesterday. We were married July 12, 1997. He died one month after our anniversary last year.

I feared it would be a day filled with the pain of his loss, but it wasn't so bad. I think the anticipation of a milestone event can often be worse than the day itself.

I woke up a little sad, but that's to be expected. I drove home alone from my vacation with the family. That took up a good 4 and ½ hours. I killed time in the car listening to talk radio, my David Sedaris book, and sometimes just drove in silence – alone with my thoughts, lots of thoughts. I was sad, no doubt, that he wasn't here with me, anticipating our anniversary date night, or weekend away, or whatever. Sad. Not devastated, just sad.

I had a hair appointment at 2 p.m., and that was a small perk. Poof! Traci got rid of the gray and we commiserated – she who had been there the morning of our wedding, with her mimosas and appetizers and magic hair skills. I remembered sitting outside in the sunshine that morning, drinking our spiked OJs and listening to my son Brandon playing the piano inside the apartment – a gift from him on my wedding morning. I left the appointment feeling a little lighter. Gray gone, young again! (I wish.) Well, younger, I guess, and widowed, and still sad, sad that Rick wouldn't be waiting outside or at home to tell me he loved my hair and how nice I looked. Sad, but I'm used to it now.

My niece Marsha offered to do anything or nothing to help me through the evening. You just never know what will make it easier. Cocooning or busyness? Trying to ignore the event, or diving in and doing some traditional activity? After gleaning suggestions from several of the widows on the Hope for Widows private group, I went with doing something Rick and I would have done together. The fact that Antman and the Wasp was released this week couldn't be a coincidence! That's where we would have been, so after a meal at our fav Mexican restaurant, Marsha and I went to the movie. I warned her in advance that she had to nudge me when Stan Lee made his cameo appearance. It's tradition. We both cracked up when he finally did.

I had a nice time. I'm thankful for Marsha, and for the other family members and friends who called or sent messages. I sent one myself, to my friend Rita. She and her late husband, Jack, shared our anniversary date. In fact, they were guests at our wedding 21 years ago, celebrating their anniversary at our reception. They would have been married 60 years this year. Jack died a few months before Rick did. The thought of what she was feeling made me sad, too.

After the movie, I decided to sit out under the gazebo with a bottle of red wine. That's where we would have ended our typical evening after any anniversary celebration, or any typical evening, for that matter. Only now, of course, Rick was no longer sitting across from me, chatting about our day. Now a small portion of his ashes are contained in the wind chime hanging above my head, and his responses as we talk are entirely in my head. After 20 years of marriage and conversation, I'm pretty sure I can fill in his parts accurately, but I so long to hear his words in my ears instead of in my mind.

And then, I chickened out. I avoided going to bed until 4am. I just couldn't do it. I knew the minute my head hit the pillow, the pain would be overwhelming. I knew the empty bed would be torture this night. I knew I couldn't compartmentalize the pain anymore.

Instead, I multitasked and avoided. I sat in my recliner, TV blasting first America's Got Talent episodes, and then political pundits in the background as I began arranging photos, blogs, and poetry into a book. This meant looking at pictures of Rick and our past, but putting a sort of veil of obfuscation between really seeing them and really feeling their impact. I can do that. Can most people? Look but not see? Look but not feel? Do as I did, and put a little veil of separation between what's in front of my face and the feelings that the photo can invoke? Of course most people can. Otherwise, when we're out in public, we'd just walk around crying in front of others, and who does that? Anyway, I just didn't want to go "there." I wanted to dull it all and avoid the pain. When I finally felt it was safe, and I was tired enough to fall asleep the second my head hit the pillow, I went to bed.

And so…this morning…meltdown time!

Just as those who avoid history are doomed to repeat it, so are those who avoid grief doomed to have it build into a tsunami. As I lay in bed, I realized I felt a bit catatonic. I didn't want to rise and do any of the things on my to-do list on this last day of vacation. I didn't have the heart or the energy to do anything – or nothing. I just lay there, zombie-like.

Why? What's wrong with me? What is it?

Oh, yes, Rick is dead, and I can't stand it anymore. I can't stand trying to go on without him. I can't stand suppressing – or even facing – the grief. I DON'T WANT THIS. I WANT HIM BACK. THIS GAME IS OVER. BRING HIM BACK – NOW!!!!

I don't want to move on. I don't want a new normal. I don't want to write my feelings, journal, bear through it, come to terms with it, accept it, face it, deal with it, live it.

I don't want him to be dead. I want someone to fix this. I want someone to wave a magic wand, stop the world, change the universe, warp time.

I want my lover back. I want to touch him, hear him, feel him, hang out with him, talk to him, share my life with him.

I WANT HIM BACK!

Stop this stupid game right now. Enough is enough. Don't tell me that I'm a whole person without him. Don't try to fool me any longer. Don't tell me I had a life before, because I don't care. Don't tell me that I have a life ahead of me, because I don't want it. I want the life I had with him. I want my lover, my friend, my partner, my soulmate. My Rick. I want our world back. I want…

I want…

I want to rage and scream and wail about this.
So I did.

Thank God the windows were closed up and the AC was on. Otherwise, they'd come cart me to the loony bin.

And so, I had my little temper tantrum. I vented my spleen, as they say. And it felt awful and good at the same time. I thought I was doing so well, thought I was "handling it." And maybe I was; maybe I am. But this morning, it all disappeared, and all the sadness in the world built up inside and spilled over.

And all the fear that I can't live without him, and the loss of everything I held dear about him, and the awful awful pain of really knowing, really getting, that I'll never ever see him or touch him or hold him again, and the longing for the comfort I felt in his arms – it all came back with a vengeance, and I raged, and I wailed, and I cried, and then…

It was over.

And here I am. Here I am.

And I have lots on my to-do list today, so I'd better get up and get going.

July 13, 2018

In Memoriam: Navigating the Bridge Between "Us" and "Me"

Ever since Rick died, when making decisions or buying something new, I've thought in terms of what he would have liked or disliked. I do lots of things "in his memory," and as the first anniversary of his death approaches, I'm slowly coming to accept that it may be time to change this way of thinking. In one more step towards adapting to my new solo life, coping with my new normal, it's time to stop making decisions based on what he liked and start figuring out my own desires. But it's still a struggle to accept that I'm no longer an "us." I'm a "me."

For instance, I hate my couch. We bought it about 15 years ago and it served its purpose, but now it's out of shape. The cushions are sloppy-looking and hang over the edge of the frame. The fabric is also a bit worn. Before he was diagnosed with lung cancer, Rick and I both decided we needed a new one, and we went to Ikea to pick out new living room furniture together. I even have pictures from the shopping trip. We opted for a couch with matching loveseat. We decided it would make the small living room look larger if we swapped out the two recliners for one love seat, yet there'd still be the same amount of seating for guests.

Then he was diagnosed and was about to start chemo, and we had more pressing concerns, so we never got around to buying it.

A few months ago, I blogged about the situation, how I had decided to go to Ikea and buy the furniture we selected together. But I still haven't done it. I had this nagging feeling that I didn't want to, and I realize now that there were several reasons for my delay.

For one thing, Rick and I had also talked about redoing the colors in the living room, repainting the walls in the same gray shade I had painted my office a couple of years ago. Would this couch and loveseat go with the new wall color? And another thing: I like sitting in a recliner and writing on my laptop in the evening. Rick never liked sitting in a recliner. Did I really want to give up the chair and replace it with the love seat?

So, about a month ago, I decided to make a bold move and see if there was anything I liked better than what we selected. I say "bold move" because even the idea of straying from what we had selected together gave me guilt pangs. But, I forged ahead and started looking, just to see if there was anything that appealed to me. And there was. I found something I like a lot.

It's not as bulky as what we chose, because the furniture I picked out with my larger-than-life husband always needed to be oversized. He was a huge man who always wanted to purchase something big and solid and comfy. When I looked at our original selection, I realized that it's the same type of couch he probably would have bought before he met me, when he was living alone. But would I have chosen this when I was a single woman? No, I would have selected something a little sleeker, like the furniture I just found. It's a mid-century modern couch, and I knew right away Rick wouldn't have liked it. The modern style would have appealed to him, but he definitely would have objected to the narrow arms – he liked (needed) a wide couch arm to rest his beefy forearms on. He most definitely would not have wanted this couch.

So finding this couch just made me more conflicted. I wanted to get the furniture we picked out together in memory of our time together, in memory of our joint decision that day at Ikea. I was planning to get what we chose when he was still here with me. How can I get something different from that choice without sacrificing his memory? Can I really pick something out for me, only me? I feel guilty about this on several levels. Because I'm considering buying something different from what we chose together, I feel like I'm losing a piece of what we shared, what we planned for our home. I'm also taking one more of those scary steps toward a future that leaves him behind. I'm choosing something for myself in my new world. I'm making a major change in "our world."

But as I pondered all these raw feelings, making this seemingly innocuous decision into a major dilemma (as I have honestly always been prone to do), I had a sudden thought, and I chuckled to myself through the tears, because I can distinctly hear what Rick would say to me right now. In Rick's voice in my head, I heard: "Honey, I'm not going to sit it in. Just get whatever you want."

Does Rick care which furniture I buy? Does he care what color the living room is? Is he really looking down on me and shaking his head vehemently over the fact that I'm buying something that appeals to me more now, as I live alone in our home? (My home?) I certainly hope that whatever our state of existence may be after death, it's not caring about the decor in our former "living" room. I'm hoping we have more important things to contemplate in our spirit life.

And that's when I realized how often I do this. I'm in Costco and there's a huge metal gazebo, and I think, when the one we have now gets old, I'm going to buy this one, because Rick really liked it and always wanted to buy it. And then I think, but he's not going to sit under it, is he? Which car should I lease next month? Rick really liked the Equinox. These new replacement cushions on our patio furniture aren't the same. Would Rick have liked them? This is the kind of mayonnaise Rick liked. This is the gas station he went to. He loved this author. He liked this restaurant. He never liked this type of music. He always wanted one of these....

For more than twenty years, I was part of an "us," part of a duo, choosing my options with another person in mind. I wanted to please my husband and he wanted to please me, and we worked it out. We chose things we both liked, both enjoyed, both wanted to share in our world.

And now I'm a "me," and I'm having a hell of a time getting used to it.

And it's not just about deciding which items to buy "in his memory." It's also about coming to terms with doing something just for myself, just for me, now that he's gone.

Last Sunday, I was cleaning up the yard, and deciding if I should buy those replacement cushions at all. I looked around at what I had accomplished and thought, wow – the yard is starting to look nice. The pool water is sparkling blue, I've cleaned out the area around the fountain, pulled the weeds, cut back the bushes, and cleaned up the deck areas. I think I'll buy those replacement cushions for the lawn chairs and maybe an umbrella for the table to replace the one that broke two years ago. After months of neglect, the yard is starting to look really pretty.

Then I became sad. I mean, who cares how nice the yard is now? It's only me here. It was different when I was fixing things up for US. I wanted to make him happy. I wanted to create a beautiful world for us – for my husband and I to share and enjoy together. And I know he did the same for me, always selecting things he knew I'd like, creating a nice space for me – the lights under the gazebo, the fountain, the flowers… when he'd finished a project, he'd take me by the hand and lead me to the yard beaming with happiness at what he'd created for our little paradise and delighted at my reaction.

How do I please just myself after living for another person all these years? How do I rectify doing things just for me?

Maybe that's what I've been trying to do, tell myself it's okay to buy the furniture if it's what we selected together. It's okay to buy OUR furniture, in memory of him, because it keeps him here somehow, keeps him alive. But it's not true, and I'm fooling myself. It's not bringing him back, and he's never going to sit in it. No matter how often I try to do something he would have liked, he's still gone, and I'm still living here alone.

Navigating this bridge between being an "us" and being a "me," is a formidable task. Can I really do things just for myself?

Choosing for myself and for myself alone is painful because with every decision, I'm forced to face reality. He is gone. He isn't coming back, so stop pretending. He won't sit on this couch, or join me in the yard. He won't eat the mayo or drive the car. It's just me now. Just my likes and dislikes, just my choices. Maybe it's time to face it: I'm here, and he's not, and I have to get used to being a "me," again.

And in my head, I can hear him encouraging me, telling me emphatically, "Honey, I love you, but I'm gone now. I don't care about any of these things anymore. Do what you want, honey. Do what YOU want."

July 21, 2018

It Takes a Village

"It takes a village to raise a child" is a well known African proverb that means child-rearing is a communal effort, that raising a child requires the experience and support of an entire community with whom the child can interact to help him or her learn and grow.

And since the death of my husband last year, I've discovered that it also takes a village to support and uplift a widow through the lowest point of her life, to assist her as she attempts to navigate her grief journey alone.

As the mother of a 30-something adult male, whenever I see a new mother trying to calm a screaming infant, a mother who looks tired and frazzled and worn out, I immediately empathize. Although it was long ago, I'll never forget the sleepless nights, the worry, the awful feeling that the world will never be safe enough for my child. I was a single mother, and I was filled with fear that I wouldn't be up to the task of raising and protecting this brand new miracle on my own. I can recall with perfect clarity the day I was released from the hospital and the fear I felt when they sent me on my way with my infant son. What have I done? How can I raise this child on my own? How will I know what to do? How can I be responsible for the life of this precious new being?

I eventually found my footing, and I raised my son to adulthood, but I couldn't have done it without my support system, my village: parents, relatives, and friends who were there for me, encouraging me and helping me along the way. But even now, years and years later, I can still remember how that new mom feels. When I see a young, tired mom with a newborn, I remember and I understand exactly what she's going through. And I wish there was some way I could tell that mom that it'll all work out, that the scary early days will pass, that she'll become a more confident mother. I'd assure her that someday her role of new mom won't be so new, and that in a few short years, she'll even get some sleep again.

In my own life, time passed and my child grew and matured, and one day, I met and married a wonderful, supportive man who took on a single mom with her 15-year-old son, and life became even better. And I'd like to think my loving and successful son turned out okay, and I'm thrilled to see him happily married and raising two children of his own.

But I'll never forget those early years of stress, and tiredness, and confusion and how I made it through with the support of my village of family and friends.

And now there's widowhood.

Over the past few months, some of my blog posts have received feedback from new widows who tell me my words describe exactly how they feel. They say things like, "My husband's been gone one month… or two months… or three months and I can't live without him, I don't know how I can go on…he was my life…my nights are empty, weekends alone are awful…friends don't understand."

And although nearly a year has passed, I'm immediately transported back to that time in my mind – the night Rick died, the weeks and first few months immediately following his death – and the fog, the confusion, and the fear and the pain, and I think, Oh you poor thing. I can relate. I get it.

When I was the mother of a newborn and I saw a mom of a teen or a young adult, I thought, Will I ever be there? Will I ever make it through teething, or the terrible twos? And in the early days after Rick died, when it was difficult to envision making it through the next hour, let alone "one day at a time," if I encountered an "experienced" widow who has survived six months of grief, or a year, or two years, or who is beginning to date, or is remarrying, or who just seems to have it all together and is successfully navigating a life alone, I would wonder, How did she do that? How did she ever get to that point? Because I will never see that. I will never ever be able to cope with this awful loss of my soulmate, the most difficult thing I have ever experienced. I have never felt pain like this, and I can't handle it. I will never sleep through the night, or feel safe, or feel whole, or feel contentment, or feel anything other than this awful, awful pain. And I certainly could never feel anything akin to joy again. My life is over. I can't go on without him.

And just as I needed the help of a village when I was a new mom, and I found support in groups like La Leche League and playdates with other parents where we hashed over the trials of motherhood, I needed to find a group who gets it, a community of other women who understand this very precise pain of losing – in an instant – your most intimate partner, the entire world the two of you have created, and the future you had planned. Having family and friends who are there for you is a blessing, and I am forever grateful for my own loving support system, but unless they've gone through this, they will never understand.

They try to be supportive, they really try, but they can't know how different this is from other deaths. It's not the same to lose a parent or a favorite aunt, a grandparent, or a friend, or a pet. I can only assume it's the same situation faced by those who have lost a child; I have no ability to understand the depth of that pain, because I haven't been there.

When I look back at how I handled "comforting" others who lost a spouse in the past, before Rick's death, I'm saddened by how inept I really must have been. I remember back and I think, oh man, what did I say to that person? I didn't get it. I had no idea. I hope I said the right things. I wish I had been more supportive. I wish I had understood how much that person needed me in the weeks and months after the funeral. How could I have been so blind to what my dad was going through when my mom died, or my aunt when she lost her husband, or even my grandmothers? How did they cope? How did they handle it on their own?

About a week after Rick died, when I was still in a fog and searching for anything at all to help me cope with the pain, someone suggested that I join a grief support group. As a web developer, I do everything online, and God knows I wasn't up to showering and dressing and leaving my house to face seeing other people, so I searched the internet and discovered that the answer was as close as Facebook: the Hope for Widows private Facebook group. Since then, I have basked in the support of other widows – people like me. Women who understand and who have undergone these same feelings, the feeling that I've lost my whole life and everything worth meaning with the death of my spouse. Women who know you don't just "get over it" and "move on" and "be grateful for the time you had" – and all those other pithy sayings that I probably imparted to the newly bereaved I've encountered in my past.

And since that fateful discovery, I have read their stories and wept with them and felt their pain. And a few times I have sought their help and advice – or just cried out to them in my suffering – and the support and the encouragement and the hugs have helped me through the heartbreak and loneliness of a long dark evening – or a lonely weekend without the man I love.

So as the first anniversary of my husband's death looms before me, that milestone that I approach with trepidation, let me publicly say thank you to those of you in my village – to those ahead of me in their journey in the Hope for Widows group. Those who have gone before and are "handling it" and who took the time to reach out – through their own pain – to reach back to me to pull me forward, or to just send me a hug or a word of encouragement. I've read your struggles and I know there is no magic pill that will take this grief away at the one year mark, so I'm more prepared for what I may encounter on this journey. I see you moving on with your lives, but still having setbacks, and I'm rooting you on as I prepare for the same in my own future. I read your triumphs and I have a glimmer of hope. By becoming a part of this village and sharing your experiences, you have helped me cope with my own grief journey, so thank you. Thank you. Thank you. I'm in awe of your resilience, ever grateful for your advice. I will never forget your kindness when I needed it most.

And to those of you who are "behind me" (now that I have nearly a year of grieving under my belt), to those who have just started out on this awful journey, who are in that initial fog state of the first weeks or first months. To you who are still in shock, still trapped between the living world that inconceivably moves on around you and the desire to remain in bed under the covers just hanging onto the memories, clinging to the shreds of the past, where your husband now resides only in your mind. To those of you who can't imagine continuing on for the next hours or weeks or months – or years – without your soulmate, or who are overwhelmed by being alone in the quiet house, or by handling all the responsibilities on your own. To those of you who have just joined this support group (the group where no one wants to be a member) – to you I say, it DOES get better.

I know it's so very hard to believe, but it does get better. I've been there. WE'VE been there, so let us help you through this. Every time you fall, we'll extend a hand and help pull you to your feet. Every time you cry out, we'll embrace you with words of support and emojis and hugs. So just keep visiting the Facebook group and reading the blog posts on the website, and utilizing any and all support offered by the Hope for Widows Foundation, because you'll find a wonderful group of women who have been there, and who get it, and who will do all they can to help you along as you travel this nightmare of a journey after the loss of your husband.

So just remember that you don't have to – and shouldn't – make this awful, overwhelming trek alone. You have the experience and support of an entire community to interact with and help you through this grief journey and, believe me, it takes a village.

August 1, 2018

The Dance

When Rick and I were first dating, I was nervous about it. We had met online and this was well before an app for swiping through potential mates was even invented. It was 1996, and it was the early days of internet dating using America Online. Because online dating was a completely new and bizarre concept, it was a scary proposition. Was it safe? Were all these men psychos, like the man from Missouri I had chatted with a month earlier, who one evening proclaimed that he wanted to "put his ex-wife back in the gutter where she belonged"? (This after telling me several different people had warned him that he had an anger problem.) I immediately ended the relationship with Mr. St. Louis and realized I had dodged a bullet that time.

The fact that Rick and I met at all still amazes me. It was about midnight and I was in an AOL chat room. I was using my new laptop, purchased using some of my inheritance from my grandmother, who had died the previous year. I was a nearly 40-year-old recent college grad with a teenaged son, and I could never have afforded that laptop on my own. I bought it with the idea of becoming a freelance writer, so it was a practical purchase, and I never dreamed I'd be using it to date.

My son and I had just moved to a small apartment, and I was working two part time jobs. One was as a secretary for a school system, but they had cut my hours in half due to budget cuts, so I went seeking an extra job using my brand new B.A. in English from the University of Michigan. Luckily, I found work as a part-time writer/editor in the evenings for an independently owned engineering training company. This is an important factor in how I met Rick five months later, at midnight on that fateful night, because it's how he found me.

AOL users had the option of whether or not to create a profile. The night before I met Rick, I realized I had not entered one for myself. When anyone tried to message me, I would never consider chatting if I couldn't get a glimpse of who that person was, so when I realized I was missing my own profile, I wrote one. The first words I used to describe myself were: writer/editor.

Rick saw that profile, and – being a writer/editor himself – messaged me. So, here are the slim odds that we met at all:

1. I have always been a night person, so being online at midnight was the perfect time for me, but Rick was a morning person, who very rarely stayed up past 10 p.m. in the entire course of our marriage. Yet he was up trolling the AOL chat rooms at midnight that night.
2. I had only the night before written a profile for myself, and only five months earlier had even become a "writer/editor" and Rick, a writer/editor himself, found me through that description. (His opening line in the chat window was actually, "I see you're a writer/editor"... smooth, eh?)
3. My new profile said I was from Garden City, Michigan, which is where my new apartment was located. Rick was living in Eden Prairie, MN, but was from...Garden City, Michigan.

It was truly miraculous that we found each other. We compared notes, and were stunned to discover that he and I already knew of each other. I had befriended his ex-wife at school, knew his kids...and had even casually run into Rick a few times when he was still living in Garden City years before. That Rick Palmer! Small world!

So, after an hour of online chatting, we switched to phone conversation. We talked every evening for the next few days until a week later, when we met in person (he was in town for his son's birthday). I knew on the first "in person" date, that he was the one. He even jokingly asked me to marry him at the restaurant, and admitted to me later in our relationship that he knew he was in love, too.

So, why was I nervous? Not because it was a man I met online, and not because we had to overcome the distance to keep up our relationship. No, I was nervous because – in only a few short weeks – I knew I was already very much in love, that I was no longer in control of my heart. At my age, relationships had come and gone, but I knew immediately that this one was different. I had found "the one," and I knew if it didn't work out, I would be devastated. I was frightened of being rejected. I was scared to death that my heart would be shattered if he left me.

I admitted this to my friend Alberta at work. I told her I was seriously thinking of not seeing him anymore! I was that afraid of rejection. I was thinking about ending the relationship with the man I already loved to "save myself" from the heartache of losing him. Self-sabotage? Maybe. But I was running scared. I hadn't had much luck in love, and escaping before it ended badly was my obviously foolish notion of how I could save myself from potential pain down the road.

I wasn't a country music fan, and Bert asked me if I had ever heard a song called, "The Dance." I hadn't. She told me it described exactly what I was so afraid of. She said, "You might miss the pain, but then you'd have to miss the dance."

I mulled that over a bit. Then, unbelievable as it may seem, something happened on our next date. Rick loved singing at karaoke bars. He had won numerous awards at bars all around the U.S. because he traveled a lot for work and sought out places to sing whenever he was in a strange town overnight. On our next date, he took me to a karaoke bar in town. I had never been to one before. Rick was called to the microphone and started singing, yup…you guessed it…The Dance.

My heart probably stopped. I'm not sure now, because it was so long ago. But how could it not? There was the man I loved, the man I was considering leaving because I was emotionally immature and scared and wanted to avoid the pain if it didn't work out – there he was singing about how awful it would be to miss the dance. And I knew right then, that I would give my life to dance with that man forever, and how foolish I had been to consider missing that dance because – risk or no risk – that's what life IS. It's dancing and loving and living. It's tossing fear aside to experience real life, real feelings, real love. Life is casting fears to the wind and experiencing whatever comes – good and bad. And life is taking a chance at love, no matter how that love might end.

And so we married, and we loved each other, and we experienced all that life threw at us for the next twenty years. We lived together through good times and through fears and failures and losses. We fought and we made up. We experienced years of joys and sorrows, births and deaths, sickness and health. We worked and played and traveled together. We renovated houses, started a business, created things. We spent holidays with our families, and vacations around the world. We laughed until our sides split and we sobbed together in each others' arms. And we spent years and years and years dancing together through the vagaries of this thing called life.

And now it's over.

And here it is, finally, the pain I wanted to avoid, the pain that I could never in my wildest dreams have imagined would be this devastating. The pain I could easily have missed if I'd cut and run to save myself in those first few months. And yes, as I feared, my heart has shattered into pieces.

But in the midst of that pain is a wealth of memories to cherish. And one of those memories takes place in a dive bar in Garden City, Michigan, in 1996, where I can still hear Rick singing, for the first time, the song he would ultimately sing – and that we would dance to – many many times throughout our marriage. And every time he sang that song, I knew. I knew that fear had almost robbed me of more than I could ever have hoped for and envisioned. And I was reminded once again that life is more than saving ourselves from pain and heartache. And every time I heard him sing those lyrics, my heart was full again and I held on tighter to the man I almost lost before we had even begun.

So, yes, I'm glad I didn't know the way it all would end, and life IS better left to chance. I could have missed this horrific pain, but I would never have experienced our beautiful, fantastic, glorious dance.

August 4, 2018

Garbage Day

Wednesday is garbage day in my part of the neighborhood, and every Wednesday evening, when I return home from babysitting my grandsons, I wheel the empty garbage can and recycling bin back to their place on the side of my garage. And – sometimes – if it's very late when I get home, or it's raining, or snowy, or for whatever reason – sometimes I wait until Thursday morning. But every week when I perform the task, every single time for the past 50 weeks, I have felt some measure of emotion – from mild sadness to a gut-wrenching pain of regret – as I pull the large plastic bins up the long driveway.

On a humid August day exactly one year ago, I uttered a simple statement that ultimately resulted in my husband's death three days later. As a last-ditch attempt to help buoy my husband's spirits, I suggested that he do a mundane chore: bring the empty garbage cans back up to the house. They were still at the curb that morning because we had been out the night before – he often wanted a late-night ice cream at McDonald's and anything that man wanted, I supplied. At this stage of his illness, he had difficulty making it up the two steps to our porch, and it was quite an ordeal helping him into the house and to his chair. For that reason, I had been too tired to retrieve the garbage bins and decided I'd do it the next morning.

So now, here we sat in our mom and pop chairs next to each other in the living room. I had just doled out his pills and injected his morning anticoagulant into his bruised and tender belly. He was drinking his Gatorade, playing on his phone, and he asked, "What's on the agenda for today, honey?"

In the past three months, he had lost 60 pounds from his 6'5" 300-pound frame. His muscular calves had eroded and his legs looked like sticks. His easy chair had been replaced by an electric lift chair that helped him to rise before he leaned heavily on a wheeled walker to begin his shaky slow pace through to other rooms of the house – always pausing to rest against the kitchen island on his way. The large, burly, muscular man I married twenty years before, the brawny guy who used to lift hundreds of pounds with little effort, who I once watched climb up and down a 16-foot ladder numerous times carrying 4×8 plywood sheets, the man who enjoyed riding his bicycle more than 10 miles a day, every day, and who walked miles each morning on vacation on the sunny beaches in Florida – the strong, invincible man I loved was now a gaunt shadow of his former self.

In the past weeks, Rick had aged twenty years. And, now that he was in remission from lung cancer, the oncologist, radiation therapist, doctors on staff at the hospital, and our primary care physician were brainstorming treatments, therapies, and ideas in an attempt to solve the problem and restore him to health.

Life was good, perfect, four months earlier. It was April, and Rick was in remission. The treatments were over, and we had a new lease on life. We went to our favorite beach on the Florida gulf to celebrate. Rick's lungs hadn't sufficiently recovered from the 39 radiation treatments, so he wasn't able to ride his bicycle, but he could take short walks. Despite a bit of breathlessness, the prognosis was good. We were both enjoying the respite from appointments, and needles, and tests, and transfusions, and all the other medical procedures involved in the fight for his life. We lived every moment to the fullest. We never missed watching a sunset or an opportunity to explore and be together and bask in the moment. Yes, life was grand because we were both aware of how fragile our existence really is, how short our time together could be, and we were taking advantage of that wake up call. We were desperate to claim and use our time together in the most meaningful way possible.

We enjoyed two weeks in Florida before he began having a chest pain in the same area where the tumors had been. We feared the cancer had returned, and drove back to Michigan, but were (mistakenly) relieved to discover there was no evidence of the cancer's recurrence.

Rick had pneumonitis, a side effect of the damage from the radiation that saved his life. It resulted in loss of appetite which caused weight loss, anemia, and weakness. He was ultimately dosed with 120 mg of steroids per day to combat the pneumonitis, and the doctors' most current thought (after weeks of puzzling over Rick's failing health) was that he had been weaned off the steroids too quickly and that was causing his current issues. Rick was fading before my eyes.

On that August morning, things were beginning to look up. Only days before, when he was released, yet again, from the hospital, he had begun a newly increased dosage of steroids, and we began to see a small increase in his appetite! At this point, we were grasping at any hope. In the two previous days, he seemed to have a little more energy, and he was less confused. There was a glimmer of the old Rick. So, yes, we were hopeful. Maybe soon things would turn around and he'd enjoy being in remission. Maybe we'd get to take his bucket list road trip across the northwest. Maybe the tumors wouldn't return – despite the looming prediction from the oncologist that they would reoccur in about 6 to 9 months as they did in 90% of small cell lung cancer patients.

So, daily, Rick practiced with his walker. His strength may have waned, but Rick was the strongest man I've ever known – for more than just his physical abilities and massive muscles. He also had a strength of will and an emotional resilience that helped him fight valiantly until there was no possible way to battle any longer. Most people would have quit long ago, but Rick rose from his bed and dressed daily, he practiced walking several feet across the front sidewalk, after I helped him down the two porch stairs by practically carrying him on my back. He walked, panting with every breath, trying to rebuild his strength. He asked me to drive him to parks, or to diners (where he picked at his meals). He tried to grocery shop, navigating the store using one of their motorized carts. He struggled down the aisles of movie theaters for our once a week date nights. He tried valiantly to continue with "normal" life when most would have succumbed to the weakness and surrendered to their beds. He tried so hard to go on with his life, despite the extreme effort required. He tried so, so hard.

And throughout the cancer ordeal, he NEVER complained. NEVER. He often said he was "lucky," because of his circumstances, because he could concentrate on his treatments without other responsibilities getting in the way. He met younger people at the chemo center who had to leave for work after treatments, or who were raising children. He often remarked, Hey, look how lucky I am – a retired 60-something who isn't burdened with work or schedules or responsibilities. He'd say, I'm so lucky that I can just get treated and go home. That I can rest whenever I need to. I'm lucky to have good medical insurance. I'm lucky I have a wife to take care of me.

Lucky.

During the chemo treatments he also said he "felt like a fraud," because after enduring four rounds of daily chemo it "only" resulted in nausea and lack of appetite (and low platelets, and blood transfusions and shots and exhaustion). He said he saw weak, emaciated cancer patients every day, yet here he was still strong and "healthy" after weeks of infusions.

His attitude kept him going. His spirit and outlook were all he had left as his body failed. And that fateful morning, exactly one year ago, when he was feeling ever so slightly stronger than he had three days before, when he was so happy that there was some improvement, and we were both so hopeful that – just maybe – things were going to keep getting better, he stopped fiddling with his phone and turned and asked, "What's on the agenda today, honey?"

And in a split second decision that I would regret the rest of my life, I came up with a chore, a simple chore, that just maybe would help the man I loved so much feel like himself again. And I said, "Hey, do you think you could bring the garbage cans up to the house?"

And I can recall with vivid detail the way his face lit up. The hope, the happiness, at my suggestion. "Yes, I can do that!" The man who was once the strongest man in the world was now excited about pushing some empty garbage bins up a driveway. And I was so happy for him. So proud of my great idea.

So hopeful.

And as he dressed to ready himself for the chore, I began my shortened workday in my home office. The family leave act had been a blessing. I worked shorter hours and was able to work from infusion centers, hospital rooms and home. I was afforded the luxury of assisting Rick through the cancer treatments and caring for him daily at home in the past months. And most of all – I was able to spend valuable time with my husband in the months before he died.

So, I went down the hall to my office, and I opened Outlook on my work laptop, and I began writing an email to my boss telling her that I saw some signs of improvement, and that I would possibly be able to come into the office for a few hours in the coming weeks because, just maybe, they had solved the problem, and, just maybe, Rick was going to start getting better.

And I heard the front door shut, and thought, Wow! He didn't even ask me to help him down the steps! And I heard the deep rattle of the empty bins. And then I heard the scream.

And three days later, Rick was dead: complications from a broken hip. Fat embolisms released from the femur and filled his already compromised lungs. He died from the complications caused by a fracture that occurred when he attempted to do a stupid chore.

And in the year since that fateful morning, I've returned the garbage cans to their place next to the garage possibly 50 times – maybe only 48 or 49 times, give or take weeks when I've been out of town, or when my nephew stopped by to cut my lawn and took them back for me. Which means that 48 or 49 times, as the wheels of the empty bins rattled up the driveway, I've replayed that scene in my living room over and over and over in my mind.

"What's on the agenda today, honey?" "What's on the agenda?"

And in the first weeks after his death, I sobbed uncontrollably. And any neighbor who glanced out a window probably wondered why the crazy widow woman was so distraught while performing the simple chore. But week after week, it got a little easier because time (and months and months of grief counseling) heals all wounds. And I still remember the words of my son one day, shortly after I expressed my guilt and regret (How could I have been so stupid? I should have known he was too weak! Why did I make the suggestion? Why? Why? Why?) And when I was done speaking, my son said, Mom, you didn't kill him. The cancer killed him.

And over the past year, week by week, on garbage day, I revisit the question. And, week after week, as I roll the cans up the drive, I repeat my mantra to myself, "The cancer killed him." "The cancer killed him." "The cancer killed him." And I rarely cry any more.

Because I know, now, that I didn't kill the man I love. I know, now, that guilt is normal, and I've accepted that hindsight is 20-20. And I also know that no amount of second guessing or regret will bring Rick back. And large, strapping men get sick, and accidents happen, and I cannot control the universe. But week by week, as I push those cans back up the driveway towards my house, I wonder if – one day in my future – garbage day will ever just be garbage day again.

August 10, 2018

The Futility of the Physical

In 1997, my husband created a logo. I was working for a man who owned a small business, and the company was developing into a formidable competitor on the market. My teenage son worked there with me, and he had just convinced the boss that we needed one of these newfangled things called websites – and had developed one showcasing our products and services. At the time, Rick and I had been together a year, and he was working in the communications department of a major union. He had won several layout and design awards for his newsletters and knew a lot about corporate identities, and one night, he took it upon himself to create a logo. The boss loved it, so it was added to the new website and product packaging, and there it remained until today.

Four years ago, our small company was purchased by a large organization. The logo was adapted slightly by adding a small line at the bottom with the new organization's name, but, otherwise, it was the same as when Rick created it more than twenty years ago. However, last month, at a departmental meeting, it was announced that our original company's identity was being completely swallowed up by the large organization. Beginning next month, the old company logo is being replaced and removed from all our products.

Very few of those present knew the history of the logo, and I'm sure they also weren't aware that this news saddened me. I thought, there goes another piece of Rick, his legacy, his mark on the world. And I swallowed the temptation to cry as business continued to be discussed around me.

And the more I contemplate this, the more I realize how hard I've tried to keep Rick alive by retaining some of his physical "stuff": the clothes, the collectibles, the things he last touched, the things he created. And little by little, as time passes, it's become more difficult to do.

The sheets he slept on had to be changed. The items he left casually on his bedside table had a year's worth of dust gathered on top and needed to be cleaned up. The sand in the car from his beach shoes on our last vacation is still there, but the car itself is a lease that I have to turn in next month. Yes, the car he selected and drove on his many days of wandering – wandering was so "him" – that car must be replaced. The last food items he purchased have gone rotten or became too old to consume. His Apple Watch stopped working and instead of repairing it, the company sent a replacement that never touched his skin, had never been near his living body, so it lost much of its meaning. I kept his phone active because it's filled with his favorite apps, his games, his e-books and music, but in the past eleven months since his death, the monthly fees are adding up to a ridiculous cost. I need to face up to the fact that I have to cancel and return the phone to Sprint.

One by one, the things he touched – the physical memorabilia – is dissipating before my eyes, because time goes on and I can't stop it. And now this, the logo being "retired," is just one more reminder of the futility of trying to hang onto Rick in the physical world. Even as I keep mementos, I think – someday, I'll probably move and leave the things he built and remodeled behind. Someday, this house will be gone. These things will have rotted and decayed. I, myself, will just be a memory. Why do I try to hang on to these physical things? It's futile.

My grief counselor broached this subject early on in our counseling sessions. She said that, eventually, I will be able to release his physical "stuff" more. That I will realize the essence of Rick, his spirit, his memory, and all he meant to me will always be in my heart. It will live there, and it will not rot or wear out or get lost or destroyed. It will ALWAYS be there, and life and time cannot take that from me.

And when he first died, I got it. I knew what she meant logically, but his stuff was still too important. Touching his shirts still made me cry. Thinking about laundering the sheets where he had last lain was overwhelming. His skin touched these sheets! His warm, living body was right in this spot! I can't do it! I can't! But I did. Eventually, I did see the futility of trying to keep a man's memory alive through a bedsheet. It can't be done. He's gone forever. The sheet didn't help alleviate the pain of his loss. The sheet needed to be laundered.

And so, a month after his death, I stripped the bed and washed the sheets. A few weeks ago, I cleared the bedside table of his last water bottle and wiped it clean. The watch was replaced by a working model. The sand in the back of the car will be returned right along with the car when I end the lease next month. His guitar, and shoes, and coats have been given away. His socks and underwear have been discarded.

And the logo will be retired next month. The logo he created. A sample of his design skills. Evidence of his talent. Physical proof that he was here. One more tangible reminder – one more piece of physical evidence that a man named Rick Palmer existed – will be gone.

Sadly, the websites he created for our clients are also slowly disappearing. One afternoon, exactly a week before his death, Rick was in his office updating a site. By then, the doctors were unable to solve the riddle of why he was continued to weaken, why his pneumonitis couldn't be cured. He was often in pain, but he got up every day, and was still trying to keep up appearances of his normal life, for me, for himself, to give us both some hope of normalcy returning and life continuing on in the blissful way it had before the diagnosis ten months before. Rick had never been one to sit around licking his wounds, although God knows, he had been fighting valiantly for some time, and I would have given up long before he did. But that afternoon, one week before his death, he worked on some website updates for a little while, then called me to join him in bed where he lay quietly, pondering something. Finally, he said, "Honey, I think we need to close the business. I'm not sure how long I'm going to live."

I protested, not because I wanted him to keep working or worrying about the business or any of that. I protested because I didn't want to hear him giving up. I didn't want to focus on all that meant. I didn't want to admit that he was truly going to die. I said I'd make a report of all our clients and we could talk more about what to do next. We never had a chance to have that discussion.

And since his death, I've been desperate to keep the business going, not for the income, but because it was ours – it was HIS. He loved design. It was his life. He had the idea of forming a web design business in 2002 so he could work doing something he loved one day after he retired. When he was offered an early retirement at age 58, he took it and developed his "side business" into a thriving company with up to 50 clients at one time.

My role had been to take care of the technical aspects of the business – setting up clients on the server, transferring websites, updating plugins, invoicing, and all that – but the bulk of the business was all Rick: he found and met with new clients, worked out their needs, and then put it all together into his beautiful, modern designs. He took photos and wrote all the content, too – it was part of our complete package. And the thought of those sites coming down, the idea that they wouldn't be forever on the internet as a testament to his talent and hard work was frightening to me, so I kept at it.

But little by little, I've had to relinquish the reins. I've cut the client list in half. I've ended the relationship with clients who required too many updates for me to keep up while performing my full-time day job. And other clients closed their doors – and their sites – because life goes on, and businesses go out of business. And as I cancel each account, and remove each site, a little part of me feels the pain and the fear that, each time I do, a part of him is being lost forever.

For the past eleven months, I've sorted Rick's things. I've clung to his possessions. I've worked on his projects. I've tried to maintain our web business – all in his memory. But I know it's a vain attempt to make time stand still. And does it matter? Will Rick's memory disappear without physical proof that he was here?

Week by week, I'm forced to accept the futility of attempting to keep him alive by surrounding myself with physical reminders, or by desperately clinging to the things he created. And those things are slowly beginning to disappear, or wear out, or fade. Some things I've relinquished by choice, but often, I have no say in the matter. It's still not easy, but it's something that cannot be avoided. Time marches on.

But despite the fact that Rick's possessions and projects and designs are steadily dwindling away, Rick did exist, and he left his legacy through his children, grandchildren, family, and friends. Rick left each of us with years and years of wonderful memories, years and years of love and laughter.

And, in the end, I know my counselor was right. As years go on, trying to keep the physical memorabilia is a futile endeavor. Rick left the imprint of his love on my heart forever, where it will never fade.

So, despite the sadness, I know I can and must loosen my grasp on the physical evidence of his existence. I know I have no choice. But, I do have one more option to keep Rick alive. I'll keep on writing his story. I'll keep on saying his name, and I'll do all I can to make sure he won't die a second time.

August 12, 2018

One Year Without You

I've been writing a lot lately. I have so many thoughts swirling around in my mind that I need to get out. I know it has to do with the looming one-year anniversary of Rick's death and the grief that evokes. I want so much to remember everything about him, his love for me, and our beautiful life together, yet thoughts of the horrible last few months of his life – watching him slowly fade away, and, ultimately, the day of his death – keep invading and causing an incredible sadness.

Mostly, I have a difficult time believing that he has been gone an entire year, that tomorrow it will be one year since that awful Sunday last August, and that it's been more than a year since we enjoyed our day-to-day life together. This poem incorporates all those frenzied thoughts from the sadness of his death to all the joyous things we shared that are absent from my life now.

One Year Without You

How can it be a year today
Since you were forced to go away?
A year without your touch, your kiss
A year alone, a year to miss…

My best friend, lover, soulmate, life –
The man who chose me for his wife,
The man who said he'd leave me never,
The one I planned to love forever.

A year ago you went away?
It's seem like it was yesterday
That you were sitting here with me,
That we were living happily.

A year without my better half.
A year without your smile, your laugh.
Oh how I miss your puns and jokes,
(And watching you drink Diet Cokes).

I can't believe it's been a year
Since hearing you say, "'Morning dear."
How do I rise for work at all
Without your daily wake up call?

Our weekday lunch dates are no more,
And weekend breakfasts are a bore.
Dinner for one is such a chore.
In bed, I long to hear you snore.

I miss our day-to-day routine,
When you would cook and I would clean.
And hearing you call out my name.
Without you, nothing is the same.

And when I get into our car
To drive around (both near and far),
I miss seeing you behind the wheel.
I still can't believe that this is real.

You used to sing around the house,
But now it's quiet as a mouse.
I miss your lovely baritone;
It's far too silent here alone.

I miss our evenings on the deck.
I miss my arms around your neck
While dancing to our favorite tune,
And kissing underneath the moon.

No skinny dipping late at night;
No one to edit what I write;
No working together on websites;
No one to hold me on cold nights.

And, oh, how you supported me:
I shed a tear, and there you'd be.
But with you gone, I'm so alone.
How have I done this on my own?

And even though it's been a year,
It's tough believing you're not here.
I'm still not used to my new life –
To being a widow, not a wife.

And 'tho you're gone, you'll always be
My husband; you're a part of me.
And one year later, on my hand
I still wear your wedding band.

I want you back; this can't be true.
I wanted much more time with you.
I sometimes dream it's all a lie,
That you're still here; you didn't die.

But no, I've had a year to face
This empty, awful, quiet place.
A year to cry, a year to grieve,
A year that's forced me to believe.

A year ago I said goodbye.
A year ago I watched you die.
A year ago our love was severed.
A year ago life changed forever.

It's been a year? Oh yes, it's true –
A long, long year of missing you.

August 13, 2018

Palmer

Richard Kevin, age 63, died Sunday, August 13, 2017, at Garden City Hospital. He was born August 23, 1953 to the late George and Emily Palmer, and is the brother of George (Cindy) Palmer. On July 12, 1997, he married Katherine Billings in Livonia. Rick was the loving father of George (Beccy) and Cindy Palmer, loving stepfather of Brandon (Lindsey) Billings, and loving "Tall Papa" to Sabastian, Taylor, Danielle, Jonas, and Stellan. Rick grew up in Garden City, Michigan.

It's Just a Day

It's just a day.

I keep telling myself that. A day has no power. A day can't hurt you. Why did I fear waking up today, August 13th? I've made it this far. I made it through all the days and weeks and months after this horrible day last year, and I've survived.

Last year, at this very time, I remember doing something dumb. I remember staring at Rick as he lay in the hospital bed unconscious, tubes and wires hooked up to IVs and monitors and oxygen. Rick was still slumped slightly towards me, despite two days of attempts by nurses to straighten him and try to make him more comfortable. I remember staring at his face and thinking…

I won't look at the calendar.

The hospital had one of those small square calendars on the wall to my left. The kind that has a very large number so the patients can easily see what day it is from their beds. I remember thinking…

But you saw it – you saw it in your peripheral vision earlier. You know you saw it: a giant number 13.

No, I told myself. I will not look. I will not see the number, and then this will be just another day. It will not be the day Rick died. The number will mean nothing, because if I don't look, this day will have no significance. If it has no significance, it means he won't die today.

Yup, crazy thoughts. One more idea about how to control life, to control the imminence of the awful, terrifying, horror I was facing. How many times as a child did I avoid stepping on those cracks in the sidewalk? I would not be responsible for breaking my mother's back. Doesn't everyone heed these superstitions? How often do we avoid breaking a mirror? Not walk under a ladder? Cross our fingers for luck? These things are proven ways to control life, aren't they? To avoid tragedy?

If I don't look at the calendar, Rick won't die.

So I didn't. It wasn't difficult to do after a while, because I couldn't take my eyes off Rick. I was trying to memorize him: his strong face and jaw, his slick bald head, his wide shoulders, his silver-haired chest, his muscular arms. I was staring at the hand I held in mine – the largest, strongest hand I had ever grasped. The hand that had held mine every single day since we fell in love, as we walked into and out of buildings, as we strolled along beaches, as we sat watching TV in the evenings – even as we drove in the car. I was staring at that hand as I clung desperately to him, willing him to live.

It was obvious by now that he would die today. His body was failing. So I leaned close and tried to hold him around all the medical paraphernalia. I put my lips to his ear and tried to whisper encouragement. I told him: Thank you, honey. I love you so much. Thank you for everything you have brought to my life. Thank you for loving me. Thank you, honey. You can go now. You can stop fighting. You can rest.

And then, a few minutes later, I changed my mind. I was NOT going to be adult about this! I don't have to! I don't want him to go! Who cares if I'm an adult woman? Who cares if I'm supposed to be mature and accept this awful fate? So, like a three-year-old stomping her foot to demand her wishes be granted, that child-woman who thought she could control the fates by not looking at a calendar took it all back. I told him, NO. I CHANGED MY MIND! NO! Don't leave me! You can't go! You can't! Please stay!

And the Rick who loved me for more than twenty years, the Rick who loved me as no other man had in my life, the Rick who knew me better than anyone – if that Rick had any conscious awareness at all – that Rick wasn't surprised by my change of heart. He was used to helping me cope with things and make difficult decisions. He was used to comforting me when life took an awful turn and I turned to him for wisdom and help. And if he was aware of his surroundings at all, deep within that unconscious state, he was smiling fondly and telling me that I had to accept this, that he was sorry that he had to go – that he had no choice.

So I held on as long as I could. Through four code blues. Through his children and the rest of his loved ones telling him goodbye. I held on through the evening, until I realized that he was still breathing, but he wasn't really there.

And then I let go. And I looked at the calendar.

August 13th.

And I knew, from that moment on, it would no longer ever be "just a day," again.

Happy Birthday to My Love

On this special day, I miss
Giving you your birthday kiss
And helping you enjoy your day
By celebrating some fun way

A movie? Dinner? Restaurant?
You'd ask, and I'd do what you want
Then rush around to find your gift
Some tech toy would give you a lift

And you were pleased so easily
Whatever gift you got from me
I loved to see your smile grow wide
When tossing the "gift wrap" aside

(Okay, I used a pillow case!)
But that put a grin on your face
And afterwards, we'd go outside
And spend our evening side by side

We'd sit outside under the stars
Out on the deck, we'd chat for hours
You'd tell your future dreams to me
What you would like your life to be

Now death has stolen you from me
And all those dreams, you'll never see
I long to share another year
To see you, touch you, have you here

Your birthdays now are in the past
The memories will have to last
My love, you won't grow old with me
You'll stay forever sixty-three

I look at photos from past years
And have no way to stop my tears
We were so happy, you and I
I miss you so much, my Big Guy

So Rick, on this your special day
I hope your spirit hears me say
My love for you will never end
And all my love to you I send

August 23, 2018

Eighty Percent Me

On my way to trivia finals this morning, I was reminded of last October, two months after Rick died, when I was invited to play with this same team in a trivia finals event. After Rick was diagnosed in October 2016, we rarely went to our regular Monday league games anymore. At first, he was often sick with chemo side effects, including low white blood counts and the risks of infection from being around too many people. Then we spent several weeks in Florida (we did play – and win – one game there). When we got back home, in the final months of his life, we were too consumed with trying to get him well again, and we didn't socialize much by then. We spent most of our time alone together.

So when I was invited to play last October, it had been a year since I had played. Rick and I had been on various teams for about ten years, and this was the first time I was going to play without him since he died.

At that early stage of mourning, I felt oddly disassociated from people and large groups. Looking back, I think it was difficult to socialize because I had nothing to say. All my mind kept repeating over and over was, "Rick's dead. Rick is gone. I can't stand this. I can't go on. I miss him. How can I live without him? Do I even want to? I miss him so much that I feel my life is over."

My obsessive thoughts were not a great topic for conversation when addressing old friends – or new acquaintances you just met playing trivia. I remember thinking I had to be brave and walk into the restaurant alone. I remember feeling like if anyone looked at me they'd immediately know something was amiss. They'd think I looked odd. They'd point and say, "She's a widow. Her husband just died. She just went through trauma."

I know in reality, no one was even focused on me, or could tell that I was filled with such emotional turmoil. It just felt that way. Like I didn't fit anywhere any more. Like I was this alien person whose other half had been ripped away. I was the victim of some type of emotional amputation and I was having great difficulty coping with daily tasks. Socializing had become work, something I must do to continue living, and something I had to get used to doing while I still felt ripped in two.

I remember sitting in the waiting room outside my grief counselor's office and looking at another woman and thinking, "I should probably try to talk to her," and making a great effort to come up with some trivial, friendly comment, some inane conversation starter. I remembered that that's what I was supposed to do in society – be polite and talk to others – but it was difficult to come out of myself; it was a great effort to break through the despondency. (And anyone who knows me, knows gabbing with a stranger was never a problem. Shutting me up would be a greater effort.)

Truthfully, at that stage of grieving, I was going out and doing things strictly to distract myself. I had no topic of interest besides my husband and my loss. Nothing gave me joy. There was no reason to leave my home, because I had no goals or direction. I simply wanted to look through old pictures, gather memorabilia, write about him, think about him, talk to his invisible presence, reminisce about him. Nothing else in life compared with the past I had enjoyed, and nothing would ever come close to holding interest to me, ever again.

After Rick's death, the only reason I did leave the house was because staying home was even more unbearable. Because sometimes I just couldn't be alone with my thoughts, anymore. Sometimes I just needed to talk to or see people. But when I did venture out, I also needed an easy escape. I rarely did anything that required me to stay more than a couple of hours. Because I knew I couldn't make it much longer without breaking out in heaving sobs, which is a real party pooper.

So I went to weddings, and parties, and dinners, and movies. But it was difficult having any interest in any of those things. In fact, I remember when I did forget about Rick for a little while, I'd be stunned! I just made it through two hours without thinking of him in any way! Wow. That was a record breaker! Because, generally, I thought about him maybe every 10 minutes – minimum. This is no exaggeration. When you've spent this long with someone, they've almost become a part of you; they're in your thoughts all the time. And the fact that this person has been permanently severed from your life is also constantly on your mind, and painfully so.

Everything elicited a memory. Everything. Because, face it, I was still in the same life circumstances I had been when he was alive. I was still doing the same types of things we did together. I was still living in the same house. Sleeping in the bed we slept in. The chair he sat in nightly was still right next to me. His place was still there at the dining room table. His cooking utensils in the kitchen. His food. His plates. His favorite glass. His trinkets and toys. Everything in the house was ours – half his. And everything reminded me of him.

And today I realized, as I awoke and readied myself to drive to trivia finals, that I am different. I'm not sure exactly when it happened, but I have slowly slowly gone from being maybe 20% myself (and 80% Rick's widow) to being 80% me, again. 80% of my life is me alone. 80% of my life is what I have created in my attempt to continue on without him. I'm nearly a whole person again. But 20% of my mind is still part of a couple, still an "us."

Rick, his memory – and his very tangible absence from my life – used to be in the very front of my mind as I attempted to go about my business throughout the day – that 80% of my existence. It's no wonder I stumbled through life: my focus was solely on him, his death, and my sadness. I couldn't see what was in front of me, because my vision was filled with my grief and my loss.

But today, I realized that there has been a great shift in my focus. It's happened so slowly that I didn't notice. Rick – and the overwhelming pain of his loss – has shifted to the back of my mind – the 20% of my thoughts. And as healthy as that probably is, that progress signals something very significant – and scary – to me.

I think I have come to realize that I have been fearing this day. I think, deep down, that I was afraid of the day when Rick wouldn't be ever-present in my mind. I feared that I – the woman who promised to love him the rest of my life – would someday survive his death, make a new life for myself, and go on without him. And I feel like I'm deserting him by moving on. I'm no longer part of our marriage. I'm moving away from our life together. I'm leaving him behind.

Twenty-two years ago, I pledged "'til death do us part," and I've heard it said that vow was completed upon his death. But, no, I didn't just vow to love him until his death; I fully intended – intend – to love him until my death, as well.

I survived another birthday without Rick two days ago, and it was somehow symbolic in my mind. It was the last "last thing." His birthday was ten days after the first anniversary of his death. I have survived an entire painful year without him, and his birthday was also the first anniversary of the night we celebrated his life. I wrote a poem in honor of him and his birthday, and when I finished, I felt a sense of something akin to relief: it's over. The first awful year of "firsts" is over.

When I woke up this morning and dressed and left for trivia finals, I was focused on the day ahead: my present, not my past. I walked into a social event without batting an eye, and I joked and talked to people with no effort – just like the old me. For the past few days, I've been making a decision about which car to lease next week. Which car do I want for me? Not for us…not based on what Rick liked (well, maybe I did think about that a little), but I'm choosing what car, and what amount of mileage, is right for me to drive in the coming two years. And for the first time since Rick died, it's okay to be making one of those major life decisions I was warned against, because it has now officially been more than a year since his death. At that significant one-year point after my husband's death, I'm supposedly in a more competent state of mind.

And this morning on the way to trivia, it hit me that I am. I think I'm going to make it. I'm 80% me again. The grief still surfaces the other 20% of the time, but it's not ever-present and it's no longer all-consuming. And it's definitely more of a painful shock when it's triggered by some memory or thought in the midst of my "return to the land of the living." But the pain also doesn't last quite as long, and I recover more quickly.

And, as usual, with anything grief-related, the awareness of this shift in my psyche is bittersweet. I'm relieved and hopeful that I have and will survive Rick's death – that I even feel interested in pursuing a life without him by my side. But I'm saddened by the knowledge that life moves on without him, because it doesn't seem like it should.

August 26, 2018

Made in the USA
Lexington, KY
06 April 2019